FROM SCHOOL TO SKY

JOSEPH'S TALE OF WAR

GEORGE HALPERN

From School to Sky
Copyright © 2021 by George Halpern

www.fromschooltosky.com
Cover Concept: Pete Fortey
Author photo: Michael Gladkey
Jewish badge on cover: photo by Daniel Ullrich

All rights reserved. No part of this publication may be reproduced, distributed, or transmitted in any form or by any means, including photocopying, recording, or other electronic or mechanical methods, without the prior written permission of the author, except in the case of brief quotations embodied in critical reviews and certain other non-commercial uses permitted by copyright law.

Tellwell Talent
www.tellwell.ca

ISBN
978-0-2288-5865-2 (Hardcover)
978-0-2288-5864-5 (Paperback)
978-0-2288-5866-9 (eBook)

for Heather Pigden-Halpern

TABLE OF CONTENTS

List of Photos vii
Foreword xi
Preface xiii
Prologue xvii
Chapter 1   "My Whole World Was Vladimir Volynsky" 1
Chapter 2   It Begins 13
Chapter 3   Operation Barbarossa—and What Came Before............. 19
Chapter 4   Battle of Moscow 23
Chapter 5   The Siege of Leningrad 27
Chapter 6   General Order 270... 30
Chapter 7   Of Parachutes and Bureaucracy 33
Chapter 8   Shot Down for the First Time.. 35
Chapter 9   Night Witches Cast Their Spell 38
Chapter 10   Big Fish.. 43
Chapter 11   Without Papers at the Movies 46
Chapter 12   From Siberia to Kolyma 49
Chapter 13   The List.. 52
Chapter 14   Life in a Dolomite Mine 54
Chapter 15   Special Training and Staying Alive 57
Chapter 16   Ambrosia 60
Chapter 17   Captured on a Special Mission.. 64
Chapter 18   The Promise 67
Chapter 19   Cigarettes Can Save your Life 70
Chapter 20   "Not One Step Back" 73
Chapter 21   The Kitten of the Volga 76
Chapter 22   Sophie... 83
Chapter 23   Kursk.. 85

Chapter 24	Fake It Till You Make It	88
Chapter 25	It's Over	93
Chapter 26	Endgame	99
Chapter 27	The "Horned Ones"	105
Chapter 28	Afterwards	113
Chapter 29	What Happened to Isabelle?	121
Chapter 30	A Promise Is a Promise	125
Chapter 31	Lots of Kids Running Around	127
Chapter 32	Your Future Country Needs You	133
Chapter 33	Time to Leave Berlin	150
Chapter 34	"I Still Won't Eat Oranges"	152
Chapter 35	"Oh, Canada"	157
Afterword		163
Acknowledgements		175

LIST OF PHOTOS

Pic 1.	Rabbi Schlomo Halevi Halpern	xv
Pic 2.	Bernard Halpern holding Joseph	xx
Pic 3.	Bernard and Ethel Halpern with son Joseph	xx
Pic 4.	Joseph's grandmother Ester Halpern (middle)	xx
Pic 5.	Joseph's maternal grandfather Lazar-David Spizman	xx
Pic 6.	Joseph's maternal grandmother Chaya Spizman	xx
Pic 7.	Joseph Halpern with sleeves rolled up with Isabell Perell (top centre) in gymnasium	5
Pic 8.	Leaders gather to sign Germany and Russia's non-aggression pact	31
Pic 9.	The Polikarpov 1-15	34
Pic 10.	The Polikarpov 1-16	34
Pic 11.	The Polikarpov Po-2	39
Pic 12.	The Night Witches collaborate	41
Pic 13.	Marina Raskova	42
Pic 14.	Irina Fyodorovna Sebrova	42
Pic 15.	Nadezhda Vasilyevna	42
Pic 16.	Yevdokiya Davidovna Bershanskaya	42
Pic 17.	Russian partisan in full fighting gear	61
Pic 18.	The Yakovlev Yak-1 a maneuverable, fast, and competitive Russian fighter aircraft	67
Pic 19.	Joseph's future wife Sophie	83
Pic 20.	Grizzly aftermath of Kursk	87
Pic 21.	Joseph Halpern formally dressed for his debut as a conductor	92
Pic 22.	Joseph Halpern by poster for the jazz concert at the Uyghur Theatre	92
Pic 23.	Raising the Russian flag over the Reichstag	103
Pic 24.	The Mustang P-51 Allied fighter plane	112

Pic 25. Joseph Stalin, Franklin D. Roosevelt, and
   Winston Churchill at the Potsdam Conference.................... 112
Pic 26. Joseph Halpern escaped from Russians in a Tupolev
   TB-3 bomber.. 116
Pic 27. Joseph Halpern in post-war Berlin.............................. 120
Pic 28. Joseph's first passionate love was Isabelle Perell......... 124
Pic 29. Head Nurse Clara Winters 130
Pic 30. Reverand Rotendorf 130
Pic 31. Dr. Fishbain 130
Pic 32. New York Mayor Fiorello La Guardia at opening
   ceremony of the Herzl Orphanage 131
Pic 33. Head Nurse Clara Winters cuts the ribbon at Herzl Orphanage...... 131
Pic 34. The rambling building housing the Herzl Orphanage........... 132
Pic 35. Joseph Halpern sets up film projectors........................ 132
Pic 36. The Hadassah Convoy Massacre 135
Pic 37. The Exodus 1947 transported 4,500 Jewish refugees ... 137
Pic 38. George Frederick "Buzz" Beurling known as
   "The Falcon of Malta" 138
Pic 39. American pilot Gideon Lichtman was first to shoot down
   an enemy plane 138
Pic 40. American Al Schwimmer (left) with David Ben-Gurion
   considered founder of the Israeli Air Force 139
Pic 41. Pilots called the jerry-rigged Avia S-199 "Messerchitts." 141
Pic 42. The Yakovlev Yak-9 142
Pic 43. American Lou Lenart led the mission......................... 144
Pic 44. Israeli Modi Alon (with sunglasses) the 101 Squadron's first
   commander 144
Pic 45. Ezer Weizsman commanded the Israeli Air Force 144
Pic 46. South African volunteer fighter pilot Eddie Cohen
   crashed and burned 144
Pic 47. Milton Rubenfeld one of the five founding pilots of
   the Israeli Air Force 145
Pic 48. Insignia of the 101 Squadron 146
Pic 49. The flying force of the 101 Squadron 148
Pic 50. Joseph Halpern working on his doctorate in Munich 151
Pic 51. The Port of Bremerhaven where Joseph and Sophie quarantined 152

Pic 52. The MS Anna Salén *brought Joseph and Sophie to Canada*........ *154*
Pic 53. Joseph's father Bernard Halpern *162*
Pic 54. Joseph's mother Ethel Halpern *162*
Pic 55. Heather Pigden when her and Joseph's love affair began *166*
*Pic 56. Heather Pigden Halpern and Joseph Halpern at home
      in Ottawa*...*174*

FOREWORD

Throughout our lives, my older brother David and I grew up hearing snippets of my father's wartime experiences. Fascinated by these stories, I thought they should be documented and preserved. Although I continued performing with my blues band, I stopped my corporate work, sold my condo in Toronto and moved in with my father and stepmother in Ottawa.

While living with my father, I spent months interviewing him to ferret out the complete story. I talked with my father regularly over several months, recording Dad's answers to systematic questions. At the end, the recordings traced my father's life before, during, and after the war. These recordings and the resulting transcriptions formed the basis of my manuscript.

Just prior to World War II, my father, Joseph Israel Halpern was a bright, athletic schoolboy in Vladimir Volynsky, Poland, a half-Jewish community. He grew up in a privileged home against the backdrop of heated discussions of the Torah (with his grandfather, a popular and well-published rabbi), wonderful cooking, laughter, and strong family ties.

Then Germany attacked Poland on September 1, 1939. Within days, Soviet Russia invaded, and Poland disappeared. Its western region became part of Germany, and Dad's Bug River area had been annexed to western Ukraine and had become Russian territory.

At first, Joseph and his friends reveled in newfound freedom: no more curfews, no more visible anti-Semitism, no more censure of unwed pregnancy (more comrades for the nation). Stalin's Russia seemed like a welcome motherland.

Sixteen-year-old Joseph, and four other boys, were soon recruited by a Russian Air Force commander and began training in gliders. "I supposed we were picked, because we all had good marks in school—especially in technical subjects like math and physics—and it was no coincidence that all five of us were in very good physical shape." Joseph said.

Dad turned his athleticism and intelligence into a brilliant career as a fighter pilot. He cheated death numerous times—by going for a smoke just before his comrades were felled by a bomb; by being able to fix motors when sent to Siberia (when he was not on "the list"); by shirking his status as "Hero of the Soviet Union" and holder of four Red Stars for bravery; and making his way to Canada and a new life. He survived by doing things of which he was not proud, while retaining his humanity and his loyalty to and love of family and his first love Isabelle.

By the end of the war, few Jewish people from Vladimir Volynsky survived: one of them was my dad. After a stint in a Displaced Persons' Camp, during which he founded the Herzl Orphanage and volunteered as a fighter pilot in the 1948 Israeli-Arab war. Dad immigrated to Canada, entering the country via Pier 21 in Halifax and onward by train to Montreal where he later re-united with his father and mother he had presumed dead—and later settled in Ottawa/Hull. As a Canadian, my dad, Joseph Halpern became a noted member of the Jewish community. At his death August 15, 2011, the *Ottawa Citizen* ran an extended news/obituary, which was picked up by Postmedia newspapers across Canada.

PREFACE

In many ways, Joseph Halpern's early life as one of the approximately 11,000-member Jewish community in Volodymyr-Volynsky (then part of Poland and renamed Vladimir Volynsky; today located in Ukraine) was typical.[1] He attended Hebrew school, lived in a kosher home, and observed Shabbat, Passover Seder, and other religious observances.

In another way, his life was unique. He lived with a grandfather who was a highly respected rabbi and scholar. The Gaon[2] and Tzadik,[3] Reb Shlomo Halevi Halpern was a very famous writer, who travelled often as he was in great demand as a lecturer. Most of his books were destroyed during the war. The book that remains ספר חומת הדת והאמונה Sefer Chomas ha-Das veha-Emunah (*The Bulwark of Religion and Faith*) is a series of drushes (talks or sermons) calling believers to cling to the traditional life of faith and resist ever-encroaching modernity.

Joseph grew up against a backdrop of endless discussion and debate about the Torah, Talmud, and the life of faith going on in his grandfather's salon (also filled with a notable religious library).

Scholars from near and far regularly crowded into his grandfather's salon. He seemed to be one whose speaking from the heart attracted ordinary believers in addition to well-educated scholars. He was seen as tender, compassionate, and brimming with love for each individual Jew. Further, Reb Shlomo Halevi Halpern was a descendent of one of the most highly respected and widely studied medieval rabbinic scholars of Europe. He was

---

[1] Incidentally, only 140 Jewish people from the city survived the Holocaust, and nearly all migrated to other countries afterwards.
[2] Goan ("genius") was an honorific often applied to rabbis as a mark of respect and acknowledgement of their greatness in Torah learning.
[3] Tzadik was a title given to righteous people considered to be spiritual masters.

known as the Mogen Avrohom (or Magen Avraham), the name of his most influential book. (Being known by the name of the most significant book was typical for highly respected rabbis). This book is a commentary which explains details of the most applicable part of the Shulchan Aruch, the most authoritative codification of Jewish religious law written in the mid-1500s.

His birth name was Avraham Abele ben Chaim HaLevi from Gombin, Poland, and he lived in the 1600s. Part of what made his commentary innovative was his incorporation of Polish customs—as a healthy Jewish community existed in Poland for over 1,000 years. In short, Joseph's grandfather descended from one of the mostly highly respected and widely studied medieval rabbinic scholars in Europe.

Warsaw, where Reb Shlomo Halevi Halpern had lived and worked for many years, was a citadel of Jewish life and learning for centuries. Kristallnacht ("the Night of Broken Glass," November 9-10, 1939), the 1939 Nazi pogrom against the Jews began and shattered this long cultural history. That night hundreds were killed, another 600 people committed suicide, and 30,000 men were sent to concentration camps. This event is viewed as the prelude to the Nazis' "Final Solution"—the murder of over 6 million Jews during the Holocaust.

Halperns come from a long line of scholars and rabbis said to be direct descendants of King David. My great grandfather, Reb Schlomo Halevi Halpern, is one of those scholars and is legendary in the Jewish community for the creation of a new way of thinking ("meta-learning")[4] for Hebrew scholars. The Warsaw of his day abounded with Jewish learning; with thousands of synagogues and centers for Torah teaching and learning, scholars young and old would fill those centers to study the word of God. At the close of business merchants and artisans would join the crowds in those centers and study into the evening hours. Only a select few could earn the recognition of the community. Rabbi Halpern enjoyed the esteem of those renowned sages and men of wisdom. He was constantly encouraged to spread his teachings and eventually became known as "Reb Schloma'leh Hamalach (translated "Reb Schlomo the angel"). Reb Schlomo traveled by train across Europe and would be greeted at each stop by crowds of eager fans anticipating his arrival. Those fans would listen intently to every word Reb Schlomo would say, often utilizing humor. In a way, he was like a comedian/scholar on tour.

---

[4] "Meta-learning" is an esoteric wisdom: the wisdom of that which is "beyond."

Rabbi Schlomo Halevi Halpern

PROLOGUE

When Joseph ran home after school, cheeks pink with fresh air tinged by the moisture of the nearby Bug River, he went to a very old house. A C-shaped structure that had withstood a century, it had undergone various modifications over the years. The main entrance sat in the centre of the two wings on a property 700 metres wide and 800 metres deep, including the border of the river. Each side of the house had a path down to the river.

The house was built by Joseph's great-grandfather. It was very light inside: outside walls had nearly floor to ceiling windows, some with window seats. Many skylights added to the abundance of natural light. Built on an angle, the skylights shed snow easily.

Surrounded by an iron fence, at the front near the road, was the main gate which had a bell that when rung, could be heard from anywhere in the house. Still, the gate was seldom locked, and people went in and out freely.

A 30-metre stone walkway led to the front door, surrounded by a garden with an abundance of flowers and trees, places to sit, and a few gazebos made of wood, iron, and other materials. People could sit on benches and enjoy different fruit trees and shrubs with the various berries: currants, red berries, and blueberries. There were roses, jasmines, lilacs, ark blue flowers that smelled good in the dark. Some just looked nice.

The gate opened to a circular driveway leading to the front door, although there were no cars (just one taxi in town), there were many horse-drawn carriages. People walked up a few steps to a white door—quite wide—like French doors, with coloured leaded glass.

Visitors rang a bell to enter, and whoever heard it went quickly to open it. There was a man who looked after the horses and kept an eye on the gate, a butler, and other household help. At that time, the family was considered wealthy and therefore had a responsibility to provide employment for others.

Guests entered a foyer, with benches where they could sit to remove galoshes and hang up outdoor clothing. When they were ready to leave, their clothing was clean and fresh, waiting for them. Cleaning up guests' soiled clothing was a practice of generosity central to Judaism.

From the foyer—up just a few steps—people entered the salon, a kind of living room, on the right. It had a grand piano and generous seating and then led through a spacious archway (which could be blocked off by a large velvet drape) to a large dining room. There, up to 24 people could be seated, for holiday gatherings and entertaining family and friends. A door connected it to the huge square kitchen (15x15 metres).

A spiral stairway led to upstairs, where there were eight bedrooms. Many people stayed over—relatives and business associates—in addition to all the family. The stairs were highly waxed and polished hardwood gleaming dark red, with carpet runners wired into place. Joseph's bedroom was simple: 5x4 metres, with a desk facing the window, a small worktable, a few shelves, and a rope outside that he used to leave the house unseen. Still higher was an attic full of stuff that Joseph enjoyed browsing through—and a place with a good view of the surroundings and of the horses grazing below.

The Rabbi's Salon

On the main floor on the left was a salon used by Joseph's paternal grandfather, Rabbi Shlomo Halevi Halpern. Snippets of discussion and debate about the Torah, Talmud, and the life of faith were a regular feature of home life. Scholars came from distances near and far to sit with the rabbi, a prolific writer and teacher, and the room was full of religious books, in addition to a large, less specialized library.

From Warsaw to the Countryside

Joseph's parents married in the early 1920s and lived in Warsaw in his grandparents' home, where Joseph was born in 1923.

Soon after Joseph's birth, his father, Bernard Halpern received a 10-year sentence for Marxist activities. Joseph and his mother, Ethel Halpern moved in with his maternal grandparents in Vladimir Volynsky: Reb Schlomo and his wife Ester Halpern joined them shortly afterwards. (It was only about five hours away by train from where Bernard Halpern was held, rather than the eight to nine hours from Warsaw). Joseph's mother visited each month and Joseph went once a year. Unlike the usual prison, it was rather resort-like—although the detainees had to pay for their "accommodations." The point was to isolate such dissidents in order to keep others from succumbing to the "disease" of their thinking.

At Home on the Estate

Basically, Joseph's maternal grandmother, Chaya Spizman ran the house, and his mother kept the books for the family import-export business. Being very fashionable, his maternal grandmother, and his mother, relied on two seamstresses for their clothing. Using French magazines that came four times a year, they designed, measured, and sewed all their clothes, dresses, and underwear. Several women worked in the home: cleaning, cooking, looking after clothing and linens. A man looked after the stoves, heating, heavy cleaning, and yard work. His grandfather, David-Lazar Spizman had a driver. His uncle Leon Spizman lived with them until he married and moved out. Using their contacts with French and German companies, they imported steel and machinery for small factories and the military. As owners of a number of woodlots, they also had people cutting and supplying wood to merchants, who in turn produced boards as building materials.

It was a kosher home—separate dishes for Passover, separate dishes for milk and for meat, and meat and milk never mixed. They slaughtered their own chickens, bought meat from a kosher butcher, and had milk and dairy products delivered daily by a local kosher farmer. A kosher baker provided bread, rolls, and bagels (and matzos for Passover)—except on weekends when his grandmother baked them herself.

The kitchen had a wood stove that had a baking oven, beside which was a cooking stove with six burners. Pots, pans, and utensils were hung from a big round grate that could be raised and lowered by a crank. Adjoining the kitchen was a huge pantry and entrance to the cellar. The cellar had stores of potatoes, carrots, and cabbages pickled in brine, salt, and garlic, and cucumbers in a salted brine with dill. Apples and pears, individually wrapped in tissue paper, were layered in sand. Grandmother's preserves: peaches, cherry jams, strawberries, wild strawberries, and every other fruit she experimented with were also stored in the cellar.

Bernard Halpern holding Joseph

Bernard and Ethel Halpern with son Joseph

Joseph's grandmother Ester Halpern (middle)

Joseph's maternal grandfather Lazar-David Spizman

Joseph's maternal grandmother Chaya Spizman

Bar Mitzvah

According to Jewish tradition, Joseph turned 13 and became a man in 1936. His family and friends celebrated his Bar Mitzvah and, after the ceremony at the synagogue, tables and chairs were set up for the upcoming celebratory feast. Hens, geese, ducks, and capons were slaughtered and fish were caught in the river Bug. Stuffed carp, meats stewed in fruit juices, ginger breads, and wines were also provided.

Traditional *pizmonim* music was played. Musicians on flutes, fiddles, accordions, cellos, and tambourines performed joyously. Usually, the cantor would begin a new song and soon everyone would join in to form a mellifluous blend of sound as if a soothing blessing surrounded them all. More Hungarian wines and brandies were imbibed as people filled their bellies with breads that Joseph's grandmother's friends had been baking for several days. Joseph gorged contently on home-cooked plum cakes, apple cakes, and honey cakes—as would any teenager, yet somehow, he felt a little different.

Earlier, robed in a brand-new navy blue suit, adorned with the talas and tefillin, he occasionally glanced up from the Torah and haftorah during the ceremony to catch a glimpse of the congregation. As he gazed at the women's side of the congregation, he witnessed tears of joy in both his mother's and grandmother's eyes. When he glanced to the men's side, he could feel immense pride emanating from each of the boys and men there; yet nothing seemed as intense as the look of gratification on his father's countenance.

During these moments he did not comprehend the importance of this stage of his life, but with maturity and necessity, it gradually became more and more clear that the lessons learned in the course of his early experiences would guide him in the future and help him survive.

Later, he watched as first women arm in arm danced in a circle. Then the men surrounded them, locking arms at the elbows and circling outside them in the opposite direction: foot stamping, with hand clapping and cheers as the men and women and the boys and the girls paired up with hips locked and a free arm swinging merrily in the air, breaking apart one by one to form a single larger circle…and so they all partied and celebrated for hours. "I became a man that day and, along with all the revelry and celebration, I knew what it was to actually feel like a man for the first time in my life." said Joseph.

CHAPTER 1

"My Whole World Was Vladimir Volynsky"

When I turned 15 on August 6, 1938, my whole world was Vladimir Volynsky. My town was located 325 kilometers southeast of Warsaw, just east of the Bug River and along the railway line between Kovel and Lemberg. Our town of about 25,000 was half Jewish and, like many Polish Jews, our family owned and ran a business.

By 1938, the Jewish population of Poland totaled 3.3 million. Poland had the largest Jewish population in Europe; second only to the United States. While Poland was the most hospitable country in Europe to members of the Jewish diaspora, it was still imperfect. Anti-Semitism had grown during the years between the first and second world wars, and Jews were blocked from many aspects of public life, including positions in government bureaucracy. However, Jews were employed in manufacturing and commerce; they owned most retail businesses and often were among the wealthiest members of their communities. Others worked as shoemakers and tailors, and in the liberal professions of medicine, education, journalism, and law.

My life as a teenager in my small Polish village was comfortable and happy. And I was deeply in love with a tomboy named Isabelle.

We had grown up together from birth; we attended the same kindergarten, same school, and the same gymnasium or high school. We lived in each other's homes, and shared grandmothers, schoolwork, friends, and fun. We climbed trees, played chess and hide and seek, made rafts, and rode horses. For Christmas Eve, we even decorated the neighbour's Christmas tree, which was lit with candles.

The street where I grew up was called *Ulica Pilsudskiego*, which the Russians later changed to *Kowelska Droga*, or *Kowelska Road*, because lying north from there about 60 kilometers was the town called Kowel. My street was located in the most affluent part of Vladimir Volynsky.

Three large properties were located on *Ulica Pilsudskiego*. Ours, the largest of the three (and in fact the largest in town), was on one side of the road. The Waintraubs' property was located directly across from it on the southwest side; occupying most of space across from us. The Perell family's property lay a little to the northwest.

Isabelle Perell and I became very attached to each other as young children. When you saw me, you saw Isabelle. Later, as we grew into teenagers, our friendship developed into young love. It was such a very special kind of love that I believe it could be experienced only by two people whose memories were as interconnected as ours. Isabelle was the love of my life.

Our mothers were friends and involved in the same charities. Our grandmothers also were great friends and they shared books, newspapers, and visits with each other. As it was in those times, my grandmother ran our estate and Isabelle's grandmother ran theirs. To me, Isabelle had been part of my life forever; my very first recollections in life by and large included her.

Isabelle was born on October 30, 1923, just about three months after me. We first met at gatherings held by our parents. As young children, we played together with toys, games, and other activities under the same adult supervision. As we grew older, our bond with each other grew exponentially stronger, so much so that we practically shared grandmothers. The Perells considered me part of their family, and Isabelle was welcomed as part of ours.

She was a real tomboy—always doing whatever I was doing, even after we began school. Fortunately for us, we started school together and were in the same class for the first two grades. We both skipped grade three, and then boy-girl segregation began. When desegregation occurred in grade seven, we continued in the same class throughout the gymnasium years until the last day of school in 1941. The Polish gymnasium system began upon completion of grade eight and was synonymous with a North American academic high school.

In the winter we skied to school together, and when the snow melted, we went on bikes. Sometimes, when the weather cooperated, we would walk the five-and-a-half kilometers to school. Isabelle and I also belonged to the same school clubs, which met at lunchtime or after class: biology club, physics club, radio club, literature club, and several others. At that time most of our lives centred on school, except in the summer—and even then, we associated with the same group of friends. Basically, school was the extension of our homes.

In the Poland of that time, school attendance was not obligatory. When we were in Hebrew school, which ended at grade eight, we had to abide by some strict rules and regulations. One of these rules stated that we could not associate with children who did not attend school. These kids usually were apprenticing to a tradesman and typically ended up working as such. One stipulation, however, was that these kids had to learn how to read and write, and there were evening courses for them to achieve this. They would learn their prospective trade during the day and learn how to read and write in the evening. Theirs was a world of which we had little understanding, and adherence to this rule typified the class distinction of the times. Without a doubt, there were definite differences among the classes—the lower working class, the middle class, and two types of upper class (not so rich and very rich).

We were not allowed to speak Yiddish at school; however, we were permitted to speak Yiddish at home. At school we would speak Hebrew or Polish. Every Jewish child could speak Yiddish as they grew up hearing their parents speaking mostly Yiddish in the home. As a matter of fact, many of the parents did not know how to speak Polish, since Germans, Hungarians, and Russians had previously occupied the territories of their home. In our part of the country there were more Ukrainians than in other parts; therefore, many of the parents spoke Ukrainian. The adults were constantly doing business with Ukrainians and vice versa. Consequently, a lot of Ukrainians spoke Yiddish, but it was considered the language of the lower class. That's just how it was. A few times I got myself into trouble at school when I was found with Yiddish books.

As we entered gymnasium together, Isabelle and I found ourselves falling in love. We kissed and hugged a lot. We would go out together often at night after curfew. We would meet up with "the gang," which consisted of a group of close friends. At first it was just five of us: the four "Golden Boys" and Isabelle. We hooked up in back alleys and amused ourselves by committing acts of harmless mischief, the basic kid prank stuff. The goal was to play a practical joke on some unsuspecting victim without meaning any real harm. We were simply amusing ourselves.

The four boys in my class who stuck together, Pipa Geller, Joseph Katz, Aaron Cantor, and myself, were known as the "Golden Boys," because of our good marks in school, our good grooming, and good clothes—and of course, our excellent manners and etiquette.

Etiquette was taught in school, with boys and girls being separated for these classes. We learned how to kiss the hands of the elderly, how to dance, how to eat properly, what to say, and how to make interesting conversation. As far as the school was concerned, we were the perfect little gentlemen. In a way, we were living double lives. Fortunately, our good reputations camouflaged our nocturnal, back-alley activities.

Isabelle had a better head for academics than I did. She learned things more easily, even though I was considered in the genius category. One incident in school stands out in my mind. In literature class, our teacher—a woman who also taught math—had given us an assignment. We were to write about any subject of our choice, as long as it was less than six pages long. Of course, when it came time a couple of days later to read our stories aloud, I had written nothing in my workbook. When asked, I stood up, proceeded to open my workbook, and pretended to read. I started my improvised story by eloquently describing a beautiful June night and segued into a problem of whether she loves me or not, while describing my lover's expressions and gestures. In the anecdote, I finally asked her to "show me her true face." I didn't have that problem with Isabelle, who truly loved me, but just thinking about it was inspiration enough for my heart-rending story. By the time I finished, my teacher was in tears, and she insisted that I provide her with a copy of my story for publication in the monthly journal distributed among all the schools. That was a challenge; however, later that night I somehow managed to recall my spoken words and wrote down my literary masterpiece. It was published and distributed among the schools.

Joseph Halpern with sleeves rolled up with Isabell Perell (top centre) in gymnasium

Each one of the "Golden Boys" now had a girlfriend, so we had grown into a group of eight, and it stayed that way right up until I left on June 22, 1941. The Russians coming in 1939 did not seem to affect our deep companionship. Despite the many changes, our bond with one another remained intact.

When the Russians arrived, life changed considerably. The authorities confiscated our estates and all state-owned properties. Since our house had all kinds of room, four Russian officers and their wives moved into our home. Isabelle's family experienced a similar fate, now hosting three Russian officers and their wives. We were not required to cook or clean for them, however; that task was left to the officers' wives. The Russian officers habitually kept to themselves and usually ate at the barracks where their troops were stationed. Occasionally, on special events, we all would be invited to the garrison with the Russians to partake of a shared festivity.

Vladimir Volynsky had been a garrison town. In the days of the Polish Army, there had been both cavalry and infantry stationed in the city, so accommodations for troops were already in place, and the townsfolk geared up to handle them. The main difference was that now they were Russian.

Living with eight Russians in our home meant some changes. Of course, all prayer was forbidden. If one dared pray, it was done in secret, but life continued and, from our point of view as teenagers, without a lot of upheaval.

The seasons passed; Isabelle and I were still inseparable. We studied together, hung out together, walked together, and talked about everything. We went to all the dances together. As a matter of fact, the very last time I saw her was when I walked her home from a school dance. It had been the last day of school activity before the summer break on June 21, 1941. By the time I kissed her goodnight, it was past two in the morning—so in fact the last time I saw her was June 22. It would not be until after the war that I would find out what happened to my beloved Isabelle.

The summer of 1938 seemed different somehow—special: a mixture of pine trees, river, and the sun on the water. We would sit on the dock, dangling our feet in sparkling water, and then dive in, feeling cool waves wrap themselves around our bodies. There was no time to stand still, as the strong current could carry us far away into the lake if we weren't careful and it was hard to swim back.

The river meandered through sun and shade. Where trees lined the banks, the water was dark green, with fingers of shadow reaching across the water. As afternoon light deepened to bronze, Isabelle's arms glowed as they emerged one after the other from the water, rhythmically reaching towards the sun and then plunging deep into dark again. Up and down, out and in, as if pulling on the sleeves of winter.

Then, in the evening of August 8, 1938, the radio news told us that Europe's ruling powers were alarmed, because Hitler had called up 1 million reserve troops. Five days later, Japan had summoned 1 million recruits. And, on the 27th, the British warned Hitler that an attack on Czechoslovakia could mean world war. Although the surface of our ordinary peaceful lives rippled, we heard our government in Warsaw tell us not to panic, that everything was under control.

About a month later, Gymnasium 232 team for which I played striker, won the Polish inter-scholastic soccer championship. We (and our entire Jewish community) were immensely proud of that victory, which turned into a great celebration at which the town mayor awarded our school a plaque of honour.

Meanwhile…Four Powers in Munich

On September 30, 1938 at a four-power conference in Munich, the leaders of France, Germany, Great Britain and Italy reached a peaceful agreement about Czechoslovakia. No Czech representative attended, under German threat of war. This pact transferred the Czech Sudeten region to Germany and guaranteed that the rest of the country would be protected against unprovoked aggression.

One autumn morning, with the air full of the smell of leaves burning in the sun and the sound of them crackling underfoot, I awakened brimming with feeling. I wanted to fly. In my dream, I was running down the meadow so fast that my outstretched arms lifted me off the ground. I felt that only my lightness made this amazing thing possible. Later, I sometimes forgot that it was a dream and thought that I actually did know how to fly, just as I knew how to breathe and to hear.

I looked around at trees so bright with reds, yellows, and oranges that the colours hurt my eyes. When I looked up, I saw the branches cutting the sky into various smaller shapes. When I turned around and around, I could barely tell what was ground and what were trees.

Neighbours greeted each other with "What a wonderful smell." as they raked the leaves into large piles—into which youngsters jumped from low-hanging branches or hid in aromatic solitude.

Isabelle said, "Raking is stupid, because the leaves continue to fall, and we have to do it all over again. But, when no leaves remain, it's an ugly time to be outside and a beautiful time to be inside looking out."

By the end of October 1938, Germany was deporting Jews to Poland. As some of these families came to live among us, we learned first-hand what it meant to be a Jew in Nazi Germany.

Lying in bed late at night, I followed the shadows of clouds passing by and watched them travel across the walls of my room—even when the curtains were closed. My dreams imitated these shadows going round and round.

The ground turned dark brown, and everything became grey and cold. The winter snow and sun had not yet come. Isabelle and I spent long periods at the window, arms around one another, quietly enjoying the warmth and the half-light of the disappearing day—and the feel of another being close, so very close.

Meanwhile…Berlin Anti-Semitism Explodes

When anti-Semitism exploded throughout Berlin on November 9, 1938, young Nazis on a rampage killed Jews at random, destroyed stores owned by Jews, and burned down hundreds of synagogues. More than 90 people, mostly Jewish merchants, were killed in that night later called Kristallnacht, "Night of Broken Glass," because of the sound of thousands of store windows being smashed. Hundreds of buildings where Jews lived and worshipped were set on fire or ransacked. Although the men killing and looting were dressed as civilians, many wore the boots of Nazi uniforms and drove party cars.

Within the month, November 27, Father Couglin—a United States radio priest of the radical right and a self-appointed apostle of the poor—used his broadcast time to claim that Jewish groups had financed the 1917 Russian Revolution. He was but one of the right-wing political thinkers whose common fodder equated communism and Jews with the "devil."

At home, Isabelle and I huddled in front of our huge fireplace ablaze with warmth—a comforting contrast with the outside world of howling wind, snow on the ground and in the air, glittering like countless diamonds in the blue moonlight. As we held each other, my spirit soared as if I too floated above amidst the stars. We later welcomed the New Year at a school dance and danced well after midnight, our usual curfew suspended for this special occasion. Despite the fabulous party, I heard people say, "Have a happy 1939." with a troubled wondering.

Meanwhile…Worldview 1939

On January 2, French Premier Daladier travelled to North Africa to investigate Italian demands for the transfer of territories. Nine days later, British Prime Minister Chamberlain met Italy's Benito Mussolini to discuss these same issues, hoping to bring Italy into the Allied sphere.

On January 17, the German government issued orders forbidding Jews to practice as chemists, dentists, and veterinarians. By February 1, Czechoslovakia ordered foreign Jews to leave within six months. Budapest declared martial law on the fourth, in the wake of the bombing of the Dohány Street Synagogue, one night earlier. It was the main synagogue.

On February 16, the German envoy in Rome asked Vatican cardinals to elect a pope who favored fascism.

On April 28, Germany offers to sign a non-aggression pact with Denmark, Estonia, Finland, Norway, Sweden and Latvia.

When we had days off school, Isabelle and I would go tobogganing. She found it scary, especially when she was in the front. Each time, she wrapped her scarf around her face until only one eye showed. Then she pulled on her gloves and tucked her sleeves into the elastic at the wrists, put her feet under the curved part of the toboggan, and divided the rope evenly between her hands. When she was in front, she screamed, "Why am I doing this?" Later she would admit that, all the way down, she was wishing that she could stop, but by then of course it was too late. But she continued to take slide after slide with me, frightened at every run.

We returned to the house covered with frozen snow that melted on the floor, pulled off our boots, and sat around the kitchen table holding mugs of hot cocoa in both hands for warmth. We found it unbelievably peaceful—as if the world had stopped for a time, everything suspended, in order to give us the gift of loving each other and enjoying those who touched our lives. The happiness within me was like a flame, glowing brighter and higher as it was fed by each moment we had together.

Meanwhile…in Prague

On March 15, Hitler demonstrated startling efficiency as his troops arrived triumphantly in Prague just eight days after they'd entered the country. Divided into regions by the invading force, the country was now controlled by the Third Reich.

Britain Pledges Support for Poland

On March 31, 1939, British Prime Minister Neville Chamberlain pledged military support for Poland in the event of any threats to her sovereignty. The official statement from London declared: "Should the Polish government feel its independence would be threatened to such an extent that it had to resist by force, Poland would find Britain and France on her side."

Events were moving quickly now. Hitler conscripted all German youth. Italian forces invaded the Kingdom of Albania on April 7, faced little resistance, and King Zog fled to Greece (one of the few countries uneasy about Mussolini's intentions). Shortly thereafter in April, the British Mediterranean fleet sailed on a mission to protect Greece and Turkey from possible attack by Italy, and Holland placed troops on the German border. The next day Hungary quit the League of Nations, and Rome conducted air raid drills. On April 28, Hitler denounced the Anglo-German naval treaty the British had proposed.

Isabelle and I were feeling intoxicated by the fresh smell of greening grass, and we spent long, lazy, blue evenings listening to songbirds and frogs. As the days gradually lengthened, the afternoon light lay thick and gold on everything we saw. We always had some time for play before supper, and we raced—Isabelle to my house or I to hers—to bike or play tennis. Walking through the ravine behind my house, we marveled at the lilies of the valley, with their small, ivory, waxen bells so perfect that they seemed surreal. We breathed deeply, trying to swallow as much of the scented air as possible. Our moments of enchantment etched themselves indelibly into my memory.

The fat purple and white globes of lilacs smelled so strong that we felt faint when we breathed them in. At twilight we lay in the grass on our backs, watching the bushes grow black into the still light sky. The first flowers that showed were the few types of forsythia on each side of our main entrance. Yellow encased in green appeared on skinny stems, and virtually overnight, the bushes were such a blaze of orange that we could see them halfway down the road.

Beneath our living room windows, dark, mossy early violets hugged the ground and, behind them, tall sticks of leaves became daffodils. Within days, tulips stood straight up—blue, red, and yellow. Behind the house, the big old trees—all of them fuzzy and green—had at their knees hard knobs of peonies with ants crawling all over them. "Licking them open." Isabelle said.

Meanwhile...Germany and Italy Unite

By May, Germany and Italy had created an "invincible block" with millions of people in one of the most grandiose alliances in modern history. On May 22, the Axis powers signed a 10-year *Pact of Steel*, binding their economies, politics, and militaries. Their declared objective was to reorganize Europe in a way that promoted the two nations and "just peace" in the world. At the ceremonial signing, officials agreed that Germany would rule on land and Italy on sea, *Mare Nostrum* (Latin for "Our Sea") in time of war which many Europeans considered imminent.

In early June 1939, 937 Jewish refugees from Germany (more than 400 of them women and children) on board the *St. Louis*, a Hamburg-American ocean liner, sailed from port to port, were denied entry into the United States, Canada, and then Cuba. By June 8, the German Reich forced all Jews in the Fatherland to join the newly-created Union of Jews.

In mid-summer, July 17, Danzig became the newest flashpoint in European tension. Hitler made it quite clear that he wanted to absorb this free port into the Reich, but both France and Great Britain had warned him that this could precipitate war. By August 23, the Nazis and the Communists shocked Western Europe by "shaking hands" in Moscow on a non-aggression treaty that stymied the efforts of London and Paris to restrain Hitler.

This treaty isolated Poland in Eastern Europe, and Hitler remained determined to annex Danzig and exact territorial concessions from Warsaw. With the new freedom to march, provided by the treaty, Hitler told military commanders to prepare for immediate action.

Things happened quickly. On September 1, General Walther von Reichenau led German troops over the dry terrain of western Poland—with no declaration of war. Two days later, France and Great Britain declared war on Germany. On September 9, German troops reached Warsaw, moving across Poland from the west, and on September 17, Russian troops pushed in from the east. Poland surrendered on September 27th, and Vladimir Volynsky became part of the Soviet Union on September 29, 1939.

CHAPTER 2

It Begins

I was born in Warsaw, Poland on August 6, 1923 (now a date shared with the anniversary of the bombing of Hiroshima), and I moved as a young child to the small Polish town of Vladimir Volynsky with my affluent family. My family consisted at that time of my Uncle Leon, my four grandparents and my mother, as my father was serving a 10-year sentence for being a Marxist. He later joined us and was part of the household during my teenage years. Reb Schlomo, my paternal grandfather died in 1935 and his wife, my grandmother Ester Halpern, passed away in 1937.

Just after I had turned 16 and was preparing to return to school after the holidays, Germany attacked Poland. It was September 1, 1939 and we were now at war. School of course was cancelled. Over breakfast in the parlor, we heard the Polish Commander Edward Rydz-Śmigły reporting every hour or so that Germany wanted the Poles to cede the Baltic port of Danzig and other Polish lands to Germany.

"Poland will be victorious and will drive those evil invaders from our homeland!" said Commander Śmigły, boasting proudly that Poland would not give the Germans even "a button off a uniform."

Later, while my parents, grandparents, and Uncle Leon speculated about these developments over lunch in the garden, I stayed by the radio. When we heard the warning siren, I ran outside and looked up into the sky. Although I could not see any planes, I felt haunted as I heard the whistle of bombs falling and the inevitable explosions that followed. My first thought was that the German bombers were trying to hit the railway lines. If so, they weren't very good at it because the railway remained intact.

Years later, however, I wondered if the Germans really did not want to hit the railroad at all, because they knew that they would need it very soon. Perhaps the bombings were just a scare tactic. Nonetheless, some houses around the railroad were hit, and a handful of families grieved those who were injured or killed.

Amazingly, people didn't seem to panic; rather they carried on with their business. The next day school remained closed and the planes came again. This time, I could identify the swastika on two bombers high in the sky. Again, the railroad was spared, but several more families suffered personal consequences. Despite our commander's rhetoric, Poland surrendered to Germany by month's end, on September 27 at 2 p.m.

Within days, many Russian planes were flying over us at a very low altitude, and I could see precisely the red star tucked under their wings. Later that day Russian tanks, trucks, and military personnel filled the streets. They told us that Poland no longer existed—its western region was now German, and our territory along the Bug River had been annexed to western Ukraine and was now Russian territory. The new border with German territory was now nine kilometers away.

Before the week ended, a group of German officials moved into a hotel in the centre of town. They said that they had come to take those who wanted to move onto the German side, and some did go. At the same time, people from the German side (mostly Jews) began arriving. This movement back and forth lasted for several weeks, until the border was closed.

One of our new government's pronouncements—and to me the most important one—was that all forms of bigotry, prejudice, and insults based on religious or racial references were to be eliminated. The new regime said that such behavior simply would not be tolerated. If reported, these incidents would mean a death penalty. During the first week, the Russians executed a dozen or so people, mostly for anti-Semitic behavior. Suddenly, everybody was getting along splendidly; everybody seemed to love everybody else, regardless of race, status, or religion.

People also began to disappear—mostly religious leaders (ministers, rabbis, and priests). Later, we heard that they had been sent to Siberia. Then, landowners began to vanish as well. Workers and/or peasants were told that the land, factories, workshops, buildings, schools, and everything else now belonged to the government (or "the people"). Everyone should take good care of all property just as an owner would, we were told.

Along with these changes, every household received a copy of Stalin's constitution and two framed portraits (one of Lenin and one of Stalin) to hang prominently in the home. Ironically, while we "new Soviets" paid nothing for the book containing the constitution, other Russian households had to pay 10 rubles for it. Stalin's government made millions this way.

Before the Soviets arrived, Poland had always had a curfew. Previously, children and youth had to wear school uniforms on school days (six days a week) and had to be off the streets after eight at night. Because I was Jewish, my day off was Saturday; for others, it was Sunday. Under the new regime, the six-day work week continued, but the day off rotated and we no longer had to wear uniforms, but most importantly for us students, we no longer had a curfew.

This new freedom was intoxicating. We had little homework, because we finished most of it at school. Suddenly, we had a lot of free time and a new sense of licentiousness. We began to party, dance, and have more sex. Many teenage girls became pregnant, and these girls were now glorified as the mothers of the future of the union. Those foolish enough to draw attention to or insult these mothers-to-be found themselves in trouble. When the pregnancy reached term, the girl would go to the hospital, give birth, and relinquish the child for adoption by the state. Then, she could choose whether to return home or volunteer in government-run nurseries so that she could be with her child.

After the Supreme Soviet Presidium's Decree of November 29, 1939, we were now Russian citizens, and everyone aged fifteen and over had three weeks to pick up a Russian passport. Afterwards, Russian officials performed random spot-checks. Those who did not have their Russian passport were sent to Siberia with their entire family. We heard of about 80 families that met this fate. Ironically, however, this worked in their favor, because a lot of them actually survived the war.

By summer of the following year, 1940, men came by truck to install a large speaker in each living room. From that day onward until I left home, the Russian radio service played from 6 a.m. until midnight. Each morning began with *Dobre utro tovarishchi* (Good morning, comrades).

We all did 10 minutes of exercises and then heard daily reports about the glory of the Motherland, along with news about its latest achievements in science, technology, manufacturing, and agriculture. These reports were punctuated by reports glorifying the Soviet leaders, primarily Stalin and other members of the *Politburo*. Every night the Russian national anthem "signed off."

We were bombarded with a constant barrage of rhetoric and proclamations about the great accomplishments by those called the "heroes of the Motherland." Radio Moscow talked continually about the five-year plan, fleshed out with reports of Russian success in agriculture and industry. We heard about the "brothers and sisters" who had completed their tasks promptly, receiving praise as "heroes of the working class." One of the earliest of these heroes was a fellow called Alexy Stakhanov, so these heroes became known as Stakhanovites. And, oh my, we heard a lot about these "heroes." It was propaganda plain and simple. We also heard many stories about Stalin, Lenin, and Marx, interspersed with some classical music. That damn radio had no "off" switch; you couldn't even control the volume! And, if you disconnected the speaker and were caught, you were shot on sight.

The installers had put the speaker in the kitchen or eating area—wherever the family was mostly likely to spend time. Only the few fortunate enough to have a bedroom with a good solid door could escape the noise. Eventually, we became so accustomed to the sound of that radio that we could partially block it out.

In Soviet fashion, everyone between the ages of 14 and 18 years was encouraged to join the Komsomol (the communist youth organization). Although not required by law, we all understood that this was not really voluntary. The few who did not join were looked down upon and basically treated as non-humans.

The schools had reopened immediately, mostly with new teachers. For me, the change was dramatic. A year before, I had been studying the Torah and learning Hebrew; now I was learning Russian and Ukrainian—and that's all we did for six months. School became difficult and confusing, as we tried to adapt to two new languages.

As we became fluent in Russian and Ukrainian, the school curriculum switched gradually to regular subjects, with a strong emphasis on the sciences. The arts component was much too slim to satisfy most students. Sports also became very important; we exercised constantly: running, playing ball, performing on overhead bars. This was called "building healthy bodies and healthy minds."

About six months into the Soviet occupation, the air force singled out some of my friends and me for training on gliders. Although it wasn't called an after-school air cadet program, that's basically what it was. Perhaps we were chosen because we all had good marks in school especially in technical subjects like math and physics, and we were all in excellent physical shape. At first, we met about three times a week, weather permitting.

Our instructors used models to teach how aircraft balance and how the rudders function. Our instructors were stereotypical Russian Air Force people—proud and stern, yet also patient and fair. They treated us as if we were regular pupils, and we enjoyed a typical trainer-student relationship. Eventually each student and an instructor would go up together in the training glider. The trainer would control the stick, but each of us placed one hand on his to develop a feel for it.

The most important part in gliding is to pick up the air current, which requires one to fly into the wind. I learned quickly and flew solo within a few weeks. The goal was to stay up as long as possible. I found this quite an adrenalin rush. But even though I always managed to keep the glider up longer that any of the other recruits, I had to land eventually.

Throughout the training, our instructor emphasized that we must report to the training facility immediately, day or night, if anything "out of the ordinary" happened. Although they never specified exactly what constituted "out of the ordinary," we knew in the early hours of June 22, 1941.

It was strange how it happened. It was just after 3 o'clock in the morning—the day after the summer solstice and the longest day of the year. Coincidently, this attack by Germany on the new Russia occurred in the morning the day after school ended, while the first attack had come on the day school was to start. On both occasions, I had attended a school dance the night before. In 1939 it had been a pre-opening school dance; in 1941, a pre-vacation school dance. I was now 17 years old.

This time, I arrived home from that dance quite late, after having taken Isabelle home—my girlfriend, my neighbour, and my very best friend. At 3:15 a.m., I was drifting off to sleep when the shelling started. This time, German artillery was bombing us from across the German side of the border just nine kilometers away. Despite the German/Soviet non-aggression pact signed in August 1939, Count von Schulenburg, the German ambassador, had handed over his government's official declaration of war at 5:30 a.m.

Now everyone in the entire town was awake. We were under artillery fire and bombs were exploding all around. Without a doubt, "something out of the ordinary" was happening; so—without even a goodbye to my family—I ran out the door, hopped on my bike, and arrived at the training facility 10 minutes later. Shortly after, more members of the glider club showed up. Finally, we were four or five in total; I can't really remember exactly amidst the excitement and rumours flying left and right.

We were to travel to the state line about six kilometers away. Our instructors loaded us on a truck, which was travelling by highway towards Kiev. By the time we reached Lutzk, it already had been bombed by German air attacks. After riding all through the night and most of the next day, we arrived at a flying field outside of Kiev.

Now we were officially annexed into the air force and immediately began training in planes with motors. No more gliders; now we were flying real planes. We were trained to fly with mortars and to shoot at targets. That's how I became a Russian fighter pilot.

That was the last I saw anybody from my town for a long time. It was much later that I discovered what had happened in my hometown or had any specific news about my family. Survivors from Ukraine who broke through the lines told us that the Germans were eliminating everyone in mass executions; they knew no more.

From then on, all I knew was that I had to find a way back home, that I had to find out what had happened to my parents, my family, and my beloved Isabelle. This desire grew daily, until it became overwhelming; I would make it happen, I thought. And my mind raced with memories of that last night together—dancing with her in my arms, her taut body against mine as I inhaled the smell of her hair, the taste of her lips when we kissed goodnight.

CHAPTER 3

Operation Barbarossa—and What Came Before

Adolf Hitler was sentenced to nine months in jail for his role in the Beer Hall Putsch, in Munich November 8, 1923. The attempted coup by right-wing members of the army and the Nazi Party was foiled by the government. Hitler was subsequently convicted of high treason. While serving his sentence Hitler wrote his political manifesto *Mein Kampf* (*My Struggle*) which was a blueprint of his agenda. Included therein was the proposition to eliminate all Jews and were details of *Lebensraum* (living space).

Between 1921 and 1925 Adolf Hitler developed the belief that Germany required *Lebensraum* in order to survive. The conviction that this living space could be gained only in the east, and specifically from Russia, formed the core of this idea, and shaped his policy after his takeover of power in Germany in 1933.

The term *Lebensraum* was coined by the German geographer, Friedrich Ratzel in 1901. Hitler's *Generalplan Ostpolicy* ("Master Plan for the East") was based on its doctrines. It stipulated that Germany required a following of Adolf Hitler's rise to power. *Lebensraum* became an ideological principle of Nazism and provided justification for the German territorial expansion into Central and Eastern Europe.

The Nazi *Generalplan Ostpolicy* was also based on its tenets. It stipulated that Germany required *Lebensraum* for its survival and that most of the indigenous populations of Central and Eastern Europe would have to be removed permanently (either through mass deportation to Siberia, extermination, or enslavement) including Polish, Ukrainian, Russian, Czech, and other Slavic nations considered non-Aryan.

Operation Barbarossa was another chance for the Germans to execute their *Blitzkrieg* ("lightning war"). *Blitzkrieg* was a form of military operation developed by an innovative member of the German military, Heinz Guderian, shortly before World War II. First used in 1940 in the successful German invasions of Belgium, the Netherlands, and France, it was a surprise attack tactic using a rapid, overwhelming force concentration that consisted of panzer units, armored, motorized and mechanized infantry formations, together with close air support. The intent was to break through the opponent's lines of defense, then dislocate the defenders, unbalance the enemy by making it difficult to respond to the continuously changing front, and defeat them in a decisive *Vernichtungsschlacht* ("battle of annihilation").

Operation Barbarossa began with over 3 million German troops, 2,500 aircraft and more than 3,000 tanks. They destroyed some 1,200 Russian aircraft in a single strike. One man, Joseph Stalin, was to blame for the enormity of the initial devastation. By purging officers in the Red Army in the 1930s, he had paralyzed the Red Army command. Then, he refused to accept the possibility of German invasion, despite the overwhelming evidence of Wehrmacht military build-up along the border. He had left his country completely vulnerable; ignoring early warnings.

Long before the German attack, word of the upcoming invasion had reached Russia. Winston Churchill, whose agents had broken the Germans' code, had cabled Stalin to warn him about Hitler's intentions. Soviet agents in Britain, United States, and even in Germany itself had confirmed that an attack was imminent. The Soviet Intelligence Network in Switzerland had identified June 22, 1941 as the attack date.

Richard Zorga, working from the German Embassy in Tokyo, verified that Germans were moving troops and placing them in strategic points near the Soviet Border. More than 3 million German soldiers were stationed along the Soviet-German border from the Baltic to the Black Sea.

Stalin's own most senior commanders, Georgy Zhukov and Semyon Timoshenko, had discussed this information with Stalin at the Kremlin. They pleaded with him for permission to give an all-border alert and install defensive positions along the border. Stalin refused, accusing them of panicky behavior and insisting that there would be no attack. Stalin's self-delusion reached criminal proportions; his lack of action allowed the Wehrmacht to destroy Soviet targets without resistance.

After the German invasion, Stalin retreated to his dacha in panic, incapacity, and shock. Realizing that he had failed and had been outwitted by Hitler, he remained stunned by the velocity of the German advances. When Stalin heard that Germany had reached Minsk in just six days, he completely lost his nerve. Overtaken by fear and denial, he stayed in isolation.

According to Zhukov's memoirs, he immediately phoned Stalin at his dacha just outside Moscow after hearing about the attack. Quoting Zhukov after reporting the situation to Stalin, "I could only hear silence." He asked Stalin, "Have you understood me? Can I have permission to return fire?" A stunned Stalin did not answer and let vital hours go by without action. Stalin finally ordered his military advisors to meet him at the Kremlin, still refusing to give the order to return fire.

Meanwhile, the Nazis bombed Russian cities and killed Soviet citizens. Panzer units swept effortlessly deep into Soviet territory, wreaking havoc upon Russia's ability to defend herself. Red Army field commanders lost control of their units. Isolated and without leadership, soldiers became dazed and surrounded, and then surrendered by the thousands. Their surrender, entangled with hundreds of thousands of fleeing citizens, created a state of disarray and confusion of colossal proportions.

Stalin remained unconvinced that reports of the attacks were genuine, or, if true, he thought they were only isolated incidents by German rogue officers acting without Hitler's knowledge. He ordered his foreign minister Vyacheslav Molotov to determine the facts. Only when Molotov confirmed the foreign press reports did Stalin give the order to fire on the Nazis. Shocked, Stalin remained in isolation, unable to face his own people; he left it to Molotov to make the official announcement.

Molotov and other members of the *Politburo* finally visited Stalin, hoping to persuade him to take command of the situation. They asked

Stalin if he would lead the defense committee, but he thought they had come to seek his resignation. Shaken by the visit, Stalin agreed, and the so-called "Man of Steel" reemerged. On July 3, he finally faced his people and addressed the nation. The same man responsible for the initial invasion and slaughter, the displacement of millions from his collectivization policies, the murder of his top generals, the massacre of the nation's intelligentsia and brilliant minds, and the order for hundreds of thousands of Soviet citizens to be shot or worked to death in slave labor camps, now called upon his people to join forces and fight a great patriotic war. His speech was filled with lies and propaganda about the Red Army's success in destroying the German's finest forces. Despite everything that had come before, his brilliance as a leader meant that Stalin still managed to galvanize his people to march to a war they believed would be over within a month and they would emerge as victors.

CHAPTER 4

Battle of Moscow

The Battle of Moscow may have been one of the most important confrontations in all of the Russia-Germany war. It was the very first victory for the Soviets and began a major change in the sense that now, Russia went on the offence. Stalin experienced, for the first time, the sweet taste of victory against Hitler; his desire to experience those same sensations of blissful delight motivated him to go aggressively at the enemy.

On November 7, 1941, thousands of Russian soldiers marched through the Red Square in Moscow, celebrating the 24th anniversary of the Bolshevik Revolution. Stalin felt the activity was needed in order to boost the sinking morale of the Russian Army (and civilians also). Meanwhile 2 million German soldiers were within 30 kilometres from the city.

When the battle was heating up, the Germans out-numbered the Russians two to one, with thousands of partisans and civilians stuck between the two armies—most of which would be killed. Against the advice of his top generals, instead of going directly towards Moscow, Hitler redirected his forces to protect his flanks. He moved Army Group North toward Leningrad and Army Group South towards Ukraine, where Hitler desperately wanted to seize the Caucasus oil fields.

This move resulted in some success for Hitler, as Army Group North managed to halt supply runs into the city and secure the "siege" on Leningrad, and Army Group South captured mineral-rich land (including Kiev) and paved a clear path to the Caucasus oil fields.

With his centre flanks secure, Hitler confidently turned his attention towards Moscow. On October 2, 1941 the Wehrmacht initiated the attack on Moscow. By utilizing strategies planned by General Field Marshal Fedor von Bock ("Bock's Plan" code-named *Operation Typhoon*), Hitler was optimistic of a quick victory. This plan called for a double-pincer movement against the Soviet Western and Reserve Fronts near Vyazma, while a second force moved to capture Bryansk to the south.

If these maneuvers were successful, German forces could encircle Moscow and compel Soviet leader Joseph Stalin to surrender. Hitler's confidence soon shrank as supply chains were interrupted. Russian resistance was more than anticipated, and unpredictable weather caused havoc among German forces. The first snow came early, on October 6, 1941; when it melted, it transformed the ground into muddy swamp-like conditions known as *rasputitsa*. Not to say that muddy terrain caused the German defeat, but just as it had done to Napoleon in 1812, this condition made advancing extremely difficult. In Germany's case, tank treads were clogged, vehicles became stuck, and infantry and horses were bogged down.

That same day Stalin recalled his top general, Georgy Zhukov from Leningrad. Ironically, general Georgy Zhukov had been removed previously from his position of chief of the general staff for suggesting that the military get out of Kiev to avoid being surrounded by the Germans. As predicted by Zhukov, this occurred. Regardless, Stalin wanted him back and immediately upon arrival on October 10, Zhukov set out to have civilians fortify Moscow. Women, elders, and teenagers were required to dig trenches and construct fortifications. More than 250,000 civilians were involved, and over 3 million tons of earth were moved. Meanwhile, Zhukov set up a defensive line over 300 kilometres long, from Kalinin in the north to Kaluga in the south, with the city of Mozhaisk in the centre. Thus, named the "Mozhaisk defence line."

In spite of many casualties, on October 27, 1941 the Germans eventually broke through the Mozhaisk line—first from the south—and soon made their way to just 35 kilometres from the capital. During this conflict, the Germans sustained human losses of around 350,000. A lot of those had to do with the Soviets deploying the newly-developed *T-34* tanks, which German tank guns and anti-tank guns had little effect on. The Russians sustained the lion's share of fatalities with over 750,000. The Germans stalled their attack a few days later, on October 31. The

Wehrmacht decided it best to wait until the supply runs were fixed and the ground froze. During this time, Muscovites moved into Metro stations, fearing imminent invasion. Babies slept in their carriages, and a library system was set up for entertainment. Many fled and, although Stalin and the highest levels of the administration and armed forces remained, many departments of government and the diplomatic corps were ordered to move to the city of Kuybyshev deeper in the interior. A large number of officials and their families also joined in the flight. Widespread looting occurred.

One week after the well-timed Bolshevik Revolution anniversary morale-boosting celebration, the ground finally froze, and the Germans resumed their attack on Moscow. Unfortunately for the Germans, the winter of 1941 was one of the coldest on record, and logistical failures rendered them unprepared. Despite enduring severe weather conditions, a lack of winter gear, frostbite, gangrene, and weather-induced mechanical failures, the Germans marched on towards Moscow. I often wondered where their inspiration and motivation came from.

The German northern Panzer unit came within 35 kilometres of Moscow but was halted by a Soviet counterattack. The southern unit, faring worse, failed to overtake or go around the well-fortified city of Tula.

The Russian forces were not stalled, and Hitler called off the attack on Moscow; German forces began to turn back. While the Germans were retreating, Stalin seized the opportunity and ordered a massive counter-offensive. By this time, over a million Russian reserves from the well-rested, battle-hardened Siberian forces had arrived. The Russians were now well organized and had plentiful supplies.

Hitler wanted to form a defence line along the entire front; his generals, however, warned against this. Hitler heeded this advice, and the German forces continued to withdraw. During this Soviet counterattack, the Germans sustained massive casualties. On three separate occasions, pockets of German forces were almost completely wiped out, and only help from the Luftwaffe air support prevented total obliteration of the Army Group Centre and the German forces.

By early January 1942, the Russians had pushed the German forces back more than 100 kilometres until stopping due to over-extension and dwindling supplies. The Germans would fight on; however, the Battle of Moscow was over, and the results of which would permanently change the entire morale on both sides—thus affecting the outcome of the war. Moscow was saved; Russia was now confidently on the offensive and the Germans (for the first time since the beginning of the conflict) were facing the revelation that they could be defeated.

CHAPTER 5

The Siege of Leningrad

Every time I landed my plane in Leningrad to deliver supplies during the siege, I experienced the feeling that I wished I could do more. The Siege of Leningrad began September 8, 1941 and lasted for a grueling 872 days in which over 1 million civilians and Soviet defenders died.

Leningrad, formally the Russian capital named Saint Petersburg and known as the "Cradle of the Great October Revolution," was the home of the Baltic Fleet and had over 600 factories, ranking second only to Moscow for industrial output. Leningrad was seen by Hitler as a symbol of communism that he wanted to destroy and then hand over any leftovers to Finland. On July 10, 1941, Hitler instructed Panzer Group 4 to launch a two-pronged attack, without waiting for the slower infantry to arrive. He did not, however, anticipate the resilience of both Leningrad civilians and Red Army forces. Several German attacks and Russian counterattacks led by General Georgy Zhukov took place. By early September 1941, the German Army Group North under Field Marshal Wilhelm Ritter von Leeb, with assistance from the Finns, surrounded Leningrad; the siege had begun.

The city council issued an order by which every person (excluding the elderly, the sick, and women who were pregnant or caring for infants) was called upon for defence work. They worked for 12 to 16 hours per day, digging over 600 kilometres of anti-tank ditches with barbed wire entanglements, constructing 15,000 pillboxes, and building 50,000 concrete blocks. Rather than engage in an all-out combat, which would have cost many German Army lives, Hitler decided instead to besiege

Leningrad, starving the population while bombarding the city with artillery fire. The city relied heavily on the importation of food, cotton, wood, coal, iron, and steel.

Rationing of electricity and bread began; within a few months, workers were given only 250 grams of bread per day and everyone else a mere 125 grams; the bread flour was mixed with sawdust. Food supplies were running out, and people began cooking grass and weeds, eating glue (wallpaper was stripped off and the potato-based glue paste was extracted). Boiling of belts and shoes became a common event, and mothers made pancakes mixed with paint to feed their children. Zoo animals were consumed early and household pets soon after. Residents burned books and furniture to keep warm. Meanwhile German incendiary bombs destroyed warehouses and morale was low. By the end of December 1941, more than 3,000 people were dying from starvation daily. Some civilians of Leningrad during the siege resorted to cannibalism. The police struggled to prevent that, so a special division to combat cannibalism was formed. It laid over 2,000 charges.

There was some relief. In early November 1941, the ice froze the surface of Lake Ladoga, snow was cleared from the western shore of the lake to Leningrad, and the "Road of Life" or *Doroga Zhizni* in Russian, was created. On November 19, 1941, Captain Mikhail Murov and his transport regiment carried the first supplies over the frozen waters. At first the ice was not that thick, and many horse-drawn wagons and trucks sank. The constant German bombardment of the roadway made for treacherous crossings. Regardless, by mid-December 1941, a railroad between the shore of Lake Ladoga and Leningrad was completed. As supplies continued to be delivered, civilians began to be evacuated, beginning with the elderly and children. Thousands of residents were evacuated; however, thousands more who remained in the city still succumbed to starvation daily. When the snow melted, barges and ships performing both duties braved German air attacks in order to deliver supplies to Leningrad and evacuate more civilians.

During the first spring of the siege, the City Soviet organized the production of vegetables wherever possible. Families, schools, factories, and offices were allocated a copy of the *Siege Gardening Handbook*, packets of seeds, and plots of land for planting.

In May 1942, fresh troops crossed Lake Ladoga to support the exhausted garrison. New defences were built inside and outside the city. These newly-constructed fortifications were not tested, however, as no major assault on Leningrad took place. The heavy bombardment on the city continued.

In January 1943, Red Army soldiers broke through the German line, rupturing the blockade and creating a more efficient supply route. Wood for insulation arrived, and eventually an oil pipeline and electric cables were laid over the lakebed. The daily death count dropped exponentially.

In early 1944, Soviet forces approached Leningrad, causing German forces to retreat southward away from Leningrad and on January 27, 1944, the "Siege of Leningrad" was over. More than 1 million Russians died during the siege. In 1945, The Soviet government awarded the "Order of Lenin" to the people of Leningrad. After the collapse of the Soviet Union in 1991, a referendum to rename Leningrad to Saint Petersburg took place on June 14, 1991. After a heated and divisive campaign, the yes side won a 54 per cent majority and, on September 6, 1991, Leningrad was officially renamed Saint Petersburg. The "Road of Life" remains a heritage site to this day.

CHAPTER 6

General Order 270

During the first two months, the Russians were completely routed. To put an end to the carnage, on August 16, 1941 Stalin issued *General Order 270*, which said: "All officers or political officials who surrendered at the front are considered traitors." They would be shot if they ever returned to the Soviet Union. Staying true to his barbaric nature, Stalin took *General Order 270* even further. Even the wives of captured officers were arrested and sent to the gulag. His own daughter-in-law served two years of hard labor. His son, Yakov Dzhugashvili, had been captured early in the war, and Stalin refused to negotiate with the enemy for his release.

Hitler expected the war to be over in six weeks, and his confidence seemed at first to be justified. Within the first two weeks, more than half a million Russians had been killed. Of the 170 Red Army divisions stationed on June 22 near the western frontier, 28 had been eliminated. The manpower and armaments of 70 more divisions had been halved. By September the enemy troops had captured Belarus, Estonia, Latvia, Lithuania, Moldavia, Ukraine, and part of Greater Russia.

Despite the German-Soviet non-aggression pact Hitler and Stalin agreed to—signed by Germany Foreign Minister Joachim von Ribbentrop and his Russian counterpart Vyacheslav Molotov—it had become increasingly likely that Germany would attack Russia. This possibility seemed clear to everyone except Stalin. No one really knows if Hitler was bluffing or if Stalin was in denial. Stalin was convinced, however, that Hitler would provoke skirmishes in order to give grounds for an invasion of Russia. Stalin was so determined not to give Hitler any justification for an attack that he forbade massive troop build-up along the border. As a result, the whole of Russia was practically unprepared for the invasion; within a month the German Wehrmacht was halfway to Moscow.

Leaders gather to sign Germany and Russia's non-aggression pact

Stalin now faced apparently insoluble problems. Several major priorities emerged: stopping the German advance; gearing the country's economy to war; mobilizing the army; evacuating everything of value for industry, farming, science, and culture from the Western regions; and defending the people.

Initially, we new pilots were flying mostly defensive missions as Russia was in a state of constant retreat. As a matter of record, more than 1,200 Russian aircraft were lost within the first nine hours of the German attack—most of them still on the ground. After one week, 90 per cent of the Soviet front-line strength ceased to exist. Hitler described the invasion as the largest military operation in history to date (and he was likely correct).

The German invading force consisted of three army groups: Army Group Centre, Army Group North, and Army Group South. Army Group Centre, which headed for Moscow, consisted of 50 divisions—15 of which had 1,630 armed planes for air support. Army Group North, with its 29 divisions (including six armored divisions and 760 planes), was advancing on the Baltic republics seeking to take Leningrad and the Soviet naval stronghold of Kronstradt. Army Group South, consisting of 57 divisions (nine armored and supported by 1,650 planes) was advancing towards Kiev and Odessa. (And, ironically, because the Treaty of Versailles required that Germany not train fighter pilots and tank operators, they had been trained in Russia).

In 1941 the German Wehrmacht had 8.5 million men, 5,639 tanks and assault guns, over 10,000 planes, and more than 61,000 guns and mortars. Its navy had 217 fighting vessels, including 161 submarines. They thought themselves invincible and justifiably so. In less than two years, the German Wehrmacht had managed to conquer Belgium, Denmark, France, Greece, Holland, Norway, and Yugoslavia; (Greece was conquered with little resistance). German morale was high.

In comparison, the Soviet Armed Forces had 5.3 million men, 1,860 new tanks (in addition to 17,000 that were obsolete), over 2,700 new planes, 67,000 guns and mortars, and a lot of outdated weaponry. Its naval force consisted of 276 warships, of which 212 were submarines. Red Army morale had been seriously undermined by the purge of officers in 1937-1938, and most civilians had suffered immense upheaval from the civil war. Consequently, Hitler felt confident that he would conquer Russia in less than six weeks. Little did he understand the resolve of the Russian people.

CHAPTER 7

Of Parachutes and Bureaucracy

We began each morning in the Russian Air Force with the mandatory consumption of a 235 ml glass (eight ounces) of vodka with breakfast, along with a toast to Stalin: "*Zo Stalina!*" I think it was a tactic to keep us brave—or at least in a state of non-concern. Separated from my fellow cadets, I was assigned to training on motor-powered aircraft, including how to fire machine guns from within the cockpit. I trained in a plane called *Polikarpov Po-2* and in a centrifuge for about four months. We practiced parachute jumping and bailing out without a parachute. By October, even though I was still in training, I had begun flying real combat missions.

One day, as we were retreating from the advancing German armies, I was stationed in a temporary airfield on an abandoned collective farm about 100 kilometers from the front near Kharkov. The weather was turning cold; I was off duty and on the ground when I heard the unmistakable sound of a *Messerschmitt Bf-109*. I looked up and saw that an air battle was about to occur a few kilometers away. Despite a few scattered clouds, visibility in the sky was good. By squinting a little, I could clearly make out two German planes flying from the west, so they were probably scouts. Three Russian pilots flying Polikarpovs were on an intercept course.

In the beginning of the war, these Russian fighter planes, called *Polikarpov 1-15* biplanes and *1-16* monoplanes, were usually not that successful in air combat. Pilots in the Spanish Civil War from 1936 to 1939 had unflatteringly nicknamed these planes "Chato," meaning flat-nosed, and "Rata," meaning rat. The biplane was constructed of an aluminum or wood frame covered by a canvas body; each of the double wings carried a swivel-mounted 7.62 mm machine gun. The pilot triggered the machine guns by pulling on either or both ropes attached to the guns. Top speed was about 360 km/h; the monoplane travelled a little bit faster. Regardless, these speeds were much slower than the German Messerschmitts whose top speed was around 570 km/h, and it didn't take much to shoot down a Polikarpov.

The Polikarpov 1-15   *The* Polikarpov 1-16

Sure enough, the plane flown by one of my comrades was hit right away. Unable to control the aircraft, he had no choice but to bail out. He jumped, and I saw his parachute open. Two of the German fighters began revolving around the escaping pilot like buzzards circling their prey with anticipation of inevitable death. My comrade was helpless. The Messerschmitts flew westward, and I heard the unforgiving rat-tat-tat sounds of machine gun fire—somewhat delayed because of the distance. This was the first time that I witnessed such brutality first-hand, and I thought to myself, "Nazi bastards!" That was the first time I remember having that thought, but I maintained it throughout the war.

The dogfight was too far away for me to determine if my comrade had been hit. When we finally found him, he was dead with dozens of bullet holes in him. I guess the Germans had orders to kill all Russian pilots. At that moment, I decided that I would never end up as a hanging target for enemy pilots. I made up my mind then and there that, if I were shot to the point of having to ground or bail out, I would not use a parachute. That is exactly what I did all four times I was shot down; each time I stayed with the plane. On one such occasion, this earned me my second "hero" award, however, no honors or awards could satisfy my ever-increasing thirst for revenge.

CHAPTER 8

Shot Down for the First Time

The first time I was shot down was quite early in the war, sometime in the fall of 1941. I am not sure of the exact date, because time took on a new meaning during those days. One usually did not know what month or day it was; we simply measured the passing of time seasonally. I figured that it was late October, because the weather was starting to get cool. It was a clear day.

We did not have a permanent base of operations, as we were constantly retreating. We were stationed in an airfield and just took off, usually in a pack of six fighters, whenever we heard the siren or the clanging of a piece of steel. Squadrons remained on standby, ready to go up instantly. Four or five, or sometimes six squadrons would take off, depending on the reports from the observation towers. We were told how many German bombers were approaching and from what direction. This information was relayed to us by telephones situated at those lookout towers. I did not envy those poor bastards enduring long shifts up in the towers, especially in winter; occasionally, some froze to death up there.

A team of enemy fighters protected approaching bombers. Usually, 10 to 12 bombers came, escorted by four fighters flying ahead or to the side of them. Our job was to engage the fighters. Usually, the fighter planes were Messerschmitts, protecting two types of bombers: the *Heinkel HE* 2 and the *Junkers JU 87* (both dive bombers). The bombers were equipped abundantly with machine guns and well-trained gunners.

Our first job was to try to shoot down the Messerschmitts. If we managed somehow to get through with some ammo left, we would shoot at the bombers. Our goal, what we had to do, was to try to hit something at any cost. First, we aimed by flying directly towards the aircraft we wanted to hit. When we got close enough, we would fire and then swerve. In order to fire both guns, you let go of the stick, causing you to go up, down, sideways, or wherever—sometimes ramming right into the bomber.

Our Polikarpovs were much slower than the German Messerschmitts. In some circumstances, this was actually an advantage. In an air fight, the enemy plane has to aim directly at you in order to get you in its sights. Because they were faster than we were, we could slow down more quickly, preventing them from having enough time to zero in. If the Messerschmitts lost too much speed, they went down. Overall, they had very little time to aim. That small advantage was all we Russians had; otherwise, it was basically a slaughter in the sky where no rules applied. Split-second reflexes meant life or death. The dogfight would continue like that for a minute or two, until the German bombers were within range of ground anti-aircraft fire. Then, we pilots disengaged and let anti-aircraft fire take over. On a good day, we took out a Messerschmitt or two; on a very good day, we shot down a bomber.

In the first few months, we lost more planes on the ground than in the air, because the German bombing raids attacked airfields before our planes could even take off. According to some statistics discovered towards the end of the war, we lost about 90 per cent of our planes in that part of the front within the first few months of the war. Nobody knew the actual number of planes destroyed; I don't think it was ever disclosed in or outside of Russia. Even as pilots, we knew very little about the strength of our own air force. We knew only what was around us. Nobody told us anything. Everything was top secret.

Now I was fully engaged in flying. On this occasion, I was in a *Polikarpov I-16,* the first Russian fighter plane with retractable landing gear, as I flew against one of the Messerschmitts; another one of our airplanes took off. Sidetracked by this for just a split second, I was hit. I think he shot through part of my tail and part of the engine, because it wasn't working. Still, there wasn't any fire or oil leaking out. While I lacked the maneuverability to control the direction, setting, or landing, while plummeting, I was able to glide down. However, the guy who hit me was still directly on my tail. Mercifully, he apparently decided that I was falling and that he needn't bother with me anymore.

Well, it was true; I was falling and couldn't slow down. Whatever the speed, it was fast enough to kill me, and I knew it. But I managed to level off for the ground approach. First, I was flying quite low over fields. I saw a hefty cluster of trees right in front of me. I didn't want to head into those trees while I was in the cockpit, because something might blow. As I flew towards those trees, I was very near to the ground, there was not enough time to hand crank the landing gear, and knew that I had to get out of the plane before crashing into them. Sinking little by little, I leveled off almost counter to the ground. I hoped my undercarriage would remain intact when I hit the ground. Thank God it did, and the impact slowed me down a bit and I just jumped out. A few seconds later, the plane lurched into the trees. It didn't blow up; it just got tangled up. I might have been okay if I had stayed with the plane, but then again, maybe not. Hitting trees doesn't give a pilot much of a chance. When my body made contact with the ground, I performed at least a dozen combinations of somersaults and bounces. Even though I was banged up a lot, I managed not to break any bones.

When I thought back afterwards about the incident, I realized that I had come very close to death. However, I had no emotional response to that fact. You just don't have time to be afraid; you cannot afford to be afraid. When flying planes, you learn very quickly to suppress all feelings of fear.

Even as a youngster growing up before the war, I had never been fearful of things that happened in life. For me, fear had to be tangible, reasonable, and logical in order for me to be afraid. But, when I found myself coming down with a plane not responding to my commands, I simply didn't have time to think about anything except coming down in one piece—surviving—and I did. Later, my natural fearless attitude would be combined with special training—including brainwashing—and I would truly believe that I was invincible.

CHAPTER 9

Night Witches Cast Their Spell

Because the whooshing sound made by their *Polikarpov P-o2* biplanes was like the sound made by a sweeping broom, the Germans nicknamed this Russian all-female 588th Night Bomber Regiment the *Nachthexe*n, or "Night Witches." They were feared and hated by the Germans to such an extent that any airman who downed one was awarded the prestigious "Iron Cross" medal. The *Polikarpov Po-2* was too small to be picked up on radar; the female pilots never used radios, so radio locators couldn't pinpoint their location either. Basically, they were like deadly ghosts.

At the onset of World War II, female pilots were barred from combat; they were originally used primarily as supporting roles and for delivering planes and supplies, etc. Marina Raskova, known as the "Soviet Amelia Earhart," combined her unmitigated determination and Stalin's desperation to change that. On October 8, 1941, after Raskova's unrelenting persuasion, Stalin gave the order to deploy three all-female air force units. These women would soon fly missions, drop bombs, and be involved in direct combat. This would be the first time, in the history of the world, that women were officially utilized in air warfare.

Raskova was in charge of recruiting. From around 2,000 applicants, she selected about 400 women for each of the three units. Most of those selected were students, ranging in age from 17 to 26. Once chosen, recruits were moved to Engels, a small town north of Stalingrad, to formally begin their training at the Engels School of Aviation. Each recruit had to train and perform as pilots, navigators, maintenance workers, and ground crew. They were expected to grasp all these skills in a fraction of the time it would usually require. As was typically the case, these brave women faced constant skepticism, sexual harassment, and grueling conditions.

The military was unprepared for women pilots, so the they received hand-me-down uniforms, including oversized boots. The *Polikarpov Po-2* biplanes were built in 1920, originally as crop-dusters and were used as training vehicles. This model aircraft, made of plywood and canvas, was a two-seater, open cockpit plane and had no protection from the elements. Flying mostly at night, pilots endured freezing temperatures, wind, and frostbite. During the harsh Soviet winters, skin could be ripped off just by touching the plane.

The Polikarpov Po-2

These older Polikarpovs had one advantage. Their maximum speed was slower that the stall speed of the Nazi planes. Ironically, this meant that the Polikarpovs could maneuver faster than the Messerchmitts, making them extremely difficult to target. Unfortunately, during combat, if hit by a tracer bullet, this wooden plane would burst into flames.

To ensure stealth, the bombing missions were done at night. The attack runs were done with three planes, the first two as decoys to draw attention and enemy fire, the third plane with a bomb tied under each wing would have to cut the engine in order to glide silently over the target and release the bombs. Getting the engine back up and running was like a "fingers crossed" affair. Many pilots possessed only a loaded pistol, as suicide was preferable to being captured.

Marina Raskova was born into the middle-class and studied music in her teens. Her father, Mikhail Malinin, was an opera star and singing instructor; her mother a teacher. Her aunt, Anna, was a famous Russian singer. Later in life Marina changed her focus to chemistry and then navigation. She became the first female navigator and pilot in the Soviet Air Force by 1933. Within a year, she became the first female instructor in the Soviet Air Force. In 1938 she, as navigator and two pilots, Polina Osipenko and Valentina Grizodubova captured the world record for the longest straight-line flight by an all-female crew. In a *Tupolev ANT* long range bomber, they flew from Moscow to Komsomol (in the far east). The flight took 26 hours and 29 minutes and covered 5,947 kilometres. Ironically, after enduring 10 days in the navigator cockpit, upon reaching their destination there was some concern about landing the plane safely. The navigator's cockpit was not a safe place to be during such an undertaking, so Raskova parachuted out of the plane before it touched down. Without her emergency kit, it took Raskova ten days to find the plane; the Tupolev had been found two days prior by a rescue crew. All were waiting for her when Raskova eventually found the plane. On November 2, 1938, all three women were decorated with the "Hero of the Soviet Union" award, the first females ever to receive this award and the only ones before World War II.

Bombing runs usually consisted of about 40 planes, with two crew in each aircraft; a pilot upfront and the navigator in the back. The weight of the bombs meant they had to fly low, making them an easier target; therefore, as previously mentioned, they flew missions only at night. The three units combined flew over 30,000 missions yet only lost 30 pilots.

The all-female 587th Bomber Aviation Regiment used twin engine *Petlyakov Pe-2* dive bombers. There were 12 commandments of the Night Witches, the first being "Be proud you are a woman." Flying attack missions were their duty, however, during their down time these heroic pilots would still do needlework, patchwork, decorate their planes, and dance. They found a secondary use for their navigation pencils as eyeliner. After all, one had to look their best while killing Germans.

The Night Witches collaborate

Another heroine among the regiments was Irina Fyodorovna Sebrova. She was a senior lieutenant and a flight commander in the all-female Night Witches during World War II. She was awarded the title "Hero of the Soviet Union" February 23, 1945 for her first 825 bombing missions; she ended up with 1,008 sorties credited. Sebrova also earned other awards; the Order of the Red Banner, the Order of the Patriotic War, the Order of the Red Star, and the Order of Lenin. Among these brave female pilots another one stood out. Nadezhda Vasilyevna Popova was a colonel and a squadron commander in the 46th Taman Guards Night Bomber Regiment during World War II. Popova achieved significant domestic publicity after completing 18 bombing sorties in one night with navigator Yekaterina Ryabova. Popova received awards for the Order of the Red Banner, the Order of the Patriotic War, the Order of Lenin, the Order of Friendship, and the Order of Honour.

When speaking about standouts among the Night Witches, one must include Yevdokia Bershanskaya who was a lieutenant colonel and commander of the 588th Regiment. After graduating from secondary school in Blagodarny, she enrolled in the Bataysk School of Pilots in 1931. After graduating, she trained other pilots from 1932 to 1939, before she was appointed as commander of the 218h Special Operations Aviation Squadron and became a deputy of the

Krasnodar City Council. She was the only woman to receive the award the Order of Suvorov. She also was awarded the Order of the Red Banner (twice), the Order of Alexander Nevsky, the Order of the Patriotic War 2nd Class, the Order of the Badge of Honor, and the Campaign and Jubilee medals.

When all was said and done, the ground-breaking all-female 588th Night Bomber Regiment dropped more than 23,000 tons of bombs on Nazi targets, flew over 30,000 combat missions and 24 members from the regiment were awarded the "Heroes of the Soviet Union." All these accomplishments while losing just 30 pilots. These brave women endured so much while making a massive contribution to defeating the Nazis. The squadron was never disbanded but was converted into the 46th Taman Guards Night Bomber Aviation Regiment which continued to fight for the Soviet Union until demobilized October 15, 1945.

Marina Raskova

Irina Fyodorovna Sebrova

Nadezhda Vasilyevna

Yevdokiya Davidovna Bershanskaya

CHAPTER 10

Big Fish

During those war years, as a pilot in the Soviet Air Force, I was shot down a total of four times and refused each time to use a parachute. Instead, I bailed out or went down with the plane before it crashed. The second time I jumped and went straight down, and when I hit the ground, I compacted both legs, cracking both above the ankles. I was picked up by ground crew and sent to the hospital, where I was x-rayed and subsequently had a cast placed on each leg. As the casts were from my ankles to just below my knees, I was able to walk with crutches within days.

While I was recuperating, I was sent to a small collective village near Rovno, where the residents raised chickens. Still in casts and walking with crutches, I arrived by train at the station, which was about five kilometers from where I was to report. A villager met me at the train station with a horse-drawn wagon and took me to report to the village elder. This elder was a kindly-looking gentleman, most likely in his 80s. He showed me my accommodations in what they called a guesthouse, but it was basically a barn with fresh hay and some blankets. He said that he would feed me this first day, and that others in the village would take turns inviting me to their respective homes for meals.

Also, he informed me I had to register in order to be allowed to stay at the guesthouse, and he directed me to a place four houses down where I should register. He said that I could find it easily because there was a sign outside that house. The elder then asked me if I wanted to work, and I replied, "Of course, I want to work." I didn't want to sit around all day doing nothing. By now it was evening and too late to register, so I went to sleep in the guesthouse/barn. Pulling a blanket over myself in the hay, I slept quite well and found it surprisingly comfortable.

The next morning, I washed with the water-filled basin provided and made my way to that house to register. Sitting royally behind a makeshift desk was a middle-aged fellow with a serious countenance and a no-nonsense attitude. When I told him my purpose, he asked me if I had a job assigned to me yet. When I replied in the negative, he said that he could not register me until I had a job assigned to me. "Fine." I said, "How do I get a job assigned to me?" He told me that I had to go about 20 houses down the main road—almost to the end of the village—to the house with a sign that read "work office" for a job assignment.

I hobbled down the street on my crutches, taking fifteen minutes to arrive at the office, where I told the proud-looking man behind the desk that I had come for a job. He asked me if I had just arrived. "Yes," I said, "I arrived yesterday." He asked me if I was registered. I told him "No, because the man who was supposed to register me told me that I needed a job before he could register me." This man, however, said, "No, that's not how it works. First, you register, then you come back and I'll give you a job."

"Fine." I said, "Are you sure?" He replied with conviction, "That's the rule."

So I hobbled back to the registration house, another 15-minute journey, and greeted the man I had met earlier. "Good morning." I said politely and told him that the other fellow said that I had to be registered before I would get a job assignment. The fellow at the registration desk said, "He doesn't know what he's talking about. Go back and tell him that I said to go ahead and give you a job first, and then I will register you!"

"That's great." I said.

Meanwhile, on the way back, a villager asked me to come into their house for something to eat. After a magnificent meal, I thanked the villager and I continued back to the work office—where I heard once again that I had to be registered first before I could be assigned a job. "That guy must be completely crazy, that son-of-a-bitch," he said, further describing him in non-complimentary words. "You go back to him and tell him to register you, and that's it! Better yet, I'll come with you!" Then he opened the top drawer in his desk, pulled out a gigantic handgun, tucked it into his belt behind his back and said, "Let's go pay him a visit."

He walked patiently with me as I hobbled, but he was cursing the comrade at the registration office all the way. I began to think that I would witness a murder before the end of the day. When we arrived at the registration office, my "escort" just laid the gun on the registrar's desk and barked, "Register him!"

"I can't register him…" the man began. The work office fellow interrupted again even more authoritatively, "Register him, I said." and reached for the gun. The registrar pulled out some papers, asked me a few questions, took my name and service number, stamped those documents, and I was registered—within two minutes. My escort picked up his gun, and we made our way back to the work office, with him patiently accommodating my pace once again. Back at the work office, he said that I would start working on a wagon that collects water from the river.

The next day, I met my mules, the ones who would be pulling the wagon. They were so uncooperative that I spent much of my time pulling, coaching, and persuading them to do their job. I would ride to the river, fill the barrels with water, and deliver them to the large chicken barn. I filled and delivered three loads each day for a few weeks, and shared meals with the villagers. The people in that village were for the most part kind and helpful and they certainly fed me well.

At the appointed time, I was sent back to the hospital by train for more x-rays, had my casts removed, and spent a few days in a hotel. For many years after, I could feel every weather change in both my legs just above the ankles, and it always reminded me of that big fish with the big gun.

CHAPTER 11

Without Papers at the Movies

At this time in 1942, we pilots were still on active duty. The Germans, however, were not very active so my squadrons weren't flying. After recuperating from my second downing in late fall, I was sent to Saratov, about 850 kilometers southeast of Moscow with a population of about 250,00 people. I was assigned to a Russian family. Families often were happy to take in Russian officers, because the household would be rewarded with all types of commodities: sugar, chocolate, tea, cigarettes, butter, and Polish or Ukrainian sausages. By this time, everything was in short supply; food was rationed and provided only monthly with the result that anything edible was greatly appreciated by the families.

The distribution system, however, was so well-organized that even items such as seeds—which were virtually impossible to acquire other than on the black market—were distributed to families that volunteered to accommodate a Russian officer. This always puzzled me, because Russia was completely surrounded by Germans, and Americans could get access only through Alaska—and yet one could find products from all over the world that had been smuggled in somehow.

One afternoon, I walked to the theatre in town and watched the movie Sun Valley Serenade featuring the Glenn Miller Orchestra, starring Lynn Bari, John Payne, Sonja Henie—the champion figure skater of the day—and Milton Berle in a cameo role. The film was shown in English with Russian subtitles and during daylight hours because of the blackouts.

When I exited the theatre, the *Militsiya*, or city police, had surrounded it. We pilots were overseen by the Communist Secret Police (NKVD). In 1934 the NKVD was known as the Peoples' Commissariat for Internal Affairs and reported to the *Politburo*. It specialized in fulfilling Stalin's desires; directly or indirectly, and hence it was responsible for the slaughter, torture, murder, and assassination of millions of individuals and families. Another policing organization, the Peoples' Commissariat for Government Affairs (NKGD), had authority to arrest both NKVD and *Politburo* members. Later, after the war, both merged into a single organization, renamed *Komitet Gosudarstvennoy Bezopasnosti*—or the KGB. In English, it means the "Committee for State Security" overseeing government affairs, foreign intelligence and the domestic security agency of the Soviet Union.

So, this night, the *Militsiya* officers were picking up and questioning people. Several officers picked me up and asked me who I was, and I said that I was a fighter pilot.

"How come you're not in uniform?" one asked.

"Well, I'm on leave." I replied. The fuller answer would have been that the Russians with whom I was billeted laundered my clothes, including my uniform; I was in civilian clothes and wasn't carrying my papers because it was just a social outing.

"Where's your army book or air force book, or whatever?" he inquired further.

"It's at the place I'm staying." I said. "If you come with me down the road a few blocks…"

"Ah…what kind of a pilot are you?" he interrupted insultingly, and then continued, "Never mind; go with the others!"

I had learned not to argue with the *Militsiya*, who were servants of Stalin's NKVD, and whose tactics of arrest, torture, enforced confession, and execution were top of mind constantly. So, I went with the others. To this day, I do not know if they really believed me, if they didn't care, or if they just needed bodies. Whenever the government needed workers for a project, the police rounded up people as required. In Russia at that time, government projects were undertaken without a mention of budget or costs, and workers were "enlisted" as needed. This time, they took us to a football field, where I shared real estate with several hundred men. It seemed more than coincidental that we all were about the same age and apparently in fairly good physical condition. We stayed in that football field for three or four days, as they collected more people—people detained for whatever reason or for any excuse—simply because workers were needed. That was just the way it was done.

CHAPTER 12

From Siberia to Kolyma

In Russia, each person knew only what he or she was "supposed" to know. If you happened to find out something you weren't supposed to know, you kept it to yourself. Nobody asked what was happening; and, in fact, if anyone did know, they wouldn't be talking about it. I was not accused of any crime, nor did I face trial. We all were just picked up; those who didn't look very strong were released to resume their normal activities. The rest of us remained like prisoners, yet we were contented enough in some ways. We shared the typical Russian attitude, which was that so long as there were guys to talk to, food to eat, and a place to sleep, no one seemed to care and nothing else mattered. We felt content because we would likely survive the day. Throughout the night, more small groups of people arrived as we slept on the grass without blankets or toilets. In the back of my mind, I was thinking, "work detail." Little did I know that I was about to experience the most barren, desolate, and northeastern regions of the USSR.

One morning they organized us into smaller groups, asked us our names, and made lists of the detainees. Being on "the list" would soon prove its importance. After taking inventory of the detainees, they loaded us on to transport trucks. Away we went to the railway station, where we were loaded into what seemed to be cattle cars in groups of about 40. In total we were about four hundred people in ten cattle wagons heading to the northeast. The train stopped repeatedly for supplies and bathroom breaks, but never at train stations; rather, at supply depots and checkpoints. Sometimes we managed to make out the names of the stations as we passed them.

Each car had a window and a door that could be opened from the inside, with a guard stationed by the door. Periodically, I looked out the window to see where we were, but mostly I couldn't tell, and it really didn't matter because the Russia of that time was a place where you were told nothing and supposed to know even less. We got used to that. We accepted that, in wartime, you basically say nothing and just do as you are told. The rest of the time you just sit and wait for things to happen.

Several times a day, the train stopped at checkpoints to load food—mostly a kind of borsch made with fish or meat. We were allowed off to go to the bathroom (even though we were supplied with buckets for that purpose in the car) and to get a bit of exercise.

About two and a half days later, we were in Novosibirsk, a big station, where we were transferred to a military train. As we travelled along for about a week, it was colder and colder at each stop. At many of the stops, groups of men were dropped off. We knew not where nor why. Then, we reached a point where they brought in winter clothing: from underwear to work-shirts, quilted jackets and pants, wool socks and hats, and felt boots (accompanied by rubbers to pull over the felt when it was wet). Thanks to 13 mm of felt, those boots were very warm, so we realized we were going into some really cold country.

At one place, we were taken to a communal bath in groups of 15. There we all had a bath, shaved, trimmed our hair, and did whatever other grooming we wished. Afterwards, we continued until we reached a place with snow on the ground. We continued our trek into colder, more snow-covered ground until we reached the final station. We knew it was the end of this particular part of the journey because the railroad tracks suddenly ended. Then we were transferred to tractor-pulled cabins. This convoy continued the odyssey with eight tractors.

These tractors were gigantic—huge machines with a thick glass-covered cab protecting the four-man crew from the elements. Each tractor pulled two huts to house the detainees and a sled that carried diesel, food, and supplies; collecting snow provided water. Mounted on skis for the journey, the cabins were about 6x4 metres. Each had a wood stove at the back, an open central area, and bunks for about 12 men along the sides. The wood was grayish, kind of like barn wood, and originally had been stained with some brown product. The wood for the sleeping quarters was plain bare planks, with straw and burlap as mattresses; they were comfortable enough to sleep on, however.

I remember thinking that it was all very well-organized. Our huts were equipped with playing cards, chess sets and other games, writing materials, and musical instruments. We made friends, told stories, played music, and danced. We were well fed and slept well, but we didn't have much room for moving around. On the way, our convoy, would occasionally stop; armed members from a cab crew would separate some people from the groups and take them out at various isolated stations where they were left behind. Once again, we had no idea why. Tractors with empty huts would turn around and others went on different routes. Eventually our tractor and cabins were alone. We passed through mountains, probably the Ural Mountains, and the trees became sparser and more stunted. Everything seemed very flat. We still had no clue as to where we were headed. We just kept going and going, it appeared to be to nowhere.

Eventually there were no trees at all; in fact, there was not much of anything. All that was visible was snow, as far as the eye could see. It was not just cold; it was freezing cold. As a matter of fact, if you spit in your hand, the saliva turned into solid ice before hitting your hand. The temperature sometimes dropped to -60, or even -70 Celsius. Anyone left outside simply wouldn't survive. There wasn't anything there: no shelter, no trees; just open space. If left exposed, a person would be dead in less than 10 minutes.

Sometime later, we stopped in a barren, desolate, and forbidding place that I later found out was called Kolyma. It was north of Siberia in the northeastern region of the Kolyma Mountains.

CHAPTER 13

The List

I soon found out that we had been sent to Kolyma to retrieve dolomite from an underground mine. The tractor stopped, and we were ordered to leave everything behind except our clothes. After we had disembarked from the huts and formed into lines, the tractor headed back the way it had come.

Inside a dome-shaped structure, I could hear the chugging sounds of a very large diesel-fueled generator. The dome was one of the few structures visible and as we approached it, we saw a door leading to an underground complex. The door was parallel to the ground, and once opened there was a ladder going down to a small compartment. Inside that small area was an open elevator shaft. A man, well-dressed for the climate, came out with a list and began calling out names. As their names were called, the men went into that chamber. Everybody went in except for me.

I was left standing there all alone, so I spoke up. "Hey! What about me?" I asked excitedly.

"Who are you?" he asked.

"Joseph." I replied matter-of-factly and told him my last name.

He looked at that list again and said, "You're not on my list."

"So." I asked him, "What am I supposed to do?"

"Go back." he said.

"What do you mean, go back?" The tractor already had turned around and was moving away. It was already so far away that I likely would have died trying to reach it. I thought quickly about making a run for it anyway, but, even if by some miracle I could have survived the run to the tractor, I had no idea if the crew would allow me in.

"Go back where?" I asked again.

"I don't care." he stated sardonically. "You don't belong here."

"Please!" I begged. "Let me into the hole and warm up, and we'll settle this thing later."

But he declined, as if he would be breaking some rule. Although I had no idea what his motive was, I simply understood that I wasn't on that dammed list and that I would die from exposure in a few minutes if he didn't let me in.

"I can't see the tractor anymore." I said to him. "I'll die out here!"

"I'm sorry but you are not on the list."

A sensation of utter hopelessness and dread filled me. Facing certain death, I had to be inventive. "I'm good with electronics." I said. This seemed to pique his interest.

"Can you fix motors?" he asked inquisitively.

"Motors…" I exclaimed emphatically, "of course I can fix motors!" He let me in.

CHAPTER 14

Life in a Dolomite Mine

Because I was the last man in the shaft, most of my comrades had already descended into our subterranean homestead, but some still remained outside the elevator door within the confines of the shelter, and we all made our way into the elevator in groups of 10 or so. The elevator descended quite slowly for about half a minute. Although I figured that we were not that deep down, I could feel the vibrations and hear the reverberating sounds from the generator. That generator was indeed powerful, as it provided all the electricity used within the mine. The walls underground had been carved out of permafrost and covered with wood. This insulation made the facility quite warm and surprisingly comfortable.

Already, people were being assigned various tasks—most delegated within the mine, which was deeper down. Another elevator led down to the mine itself. Although I never worked down there, I did venture below into it for a gander every now and then. The miners' working conditions were quite good. As opposed to coal mining, dolomite mines require less structural support and, although there was no forest nearby, the wood supply was plentiful. No blasting was required. The miners simply drilled holes and used a machine to extract and crush the payload. Every few meters, they constructed wooden supports and installed lights. And, so it went. This rare form of dolomite, found only at this location and a few other far-flung geographical sites, was mixed with steel to strengthen it.

The man with the list introduced me to another supervisor who, after being told of my motor-repairing capabilities, reluctantly took charge of me and led me to a spacious work station filled with defunct motors of all shapes and sizes: motors for the drills, for the conveyer belts, for the generator, and for all sorts of other things. This was to be my new home. Although it had sleeping quarters for three people, I was the only occupant. Quite quickly, I noticed the abundant supply of jars filled with shellac—and immediately experienced a craving for vodka. I knew that the shellac, which was used to seal the components of the motors, contained a large volume of alcohol, and I had become accustomed to a glass of vodka for breakfast, as was the custom in the air force.

I was now assigned to the workshop, and as my first task, I looked around and found a supply area, and then procured enough materials (including some copper tubes) to make a still. I heated up the shellac, distilled the alcohol, and ended up with a continuous source of decent quality hooch. One of the skills learned early in Russian life is to distinguish good alcohol from bad, and I had quickly learned that ability. Needless to say, I became very popular at that dolomite mine. As a matter of record, the first few guys to taste my brew actually kissed me. I also repaired many of those broken motors and was appreciated for that as well.

My new life in the mine, very much like a prison sentence, quickly became routine. We were wakened for a breakfast of bread and tea or coffee at 6 a.m. We all worked long hours with few breaks except for lunch and dinner, mostly a borsch made with meat or fish, a common meal in all of the armed forces. The men worked hard, so the portions were large; we were well fed.

Although we had little free time, there was a recreation area with two phonographs and a few 78-rpm records—and an abundant stockpile of books about Stalin and other heroes of the Motherland. We had access to letter-writing materials, and many spent time writing and sending letters. Who knows, however, if any of these letters actually reached their destination or were even mailed. I don't remember any new workers (or letters) arriving during my stay.

Periodically, provision transports arrived about every three weeks or so, but no new workers came while I was there. The replenishments were mostly food, diesel, timber, and other provisions to keep the place going, and of course a barrel of shellac. Once supplies were unloaded, the transport tractors were reloaded with the freshly mined dolomite and away they went.

My claim to being a fighter pilot continued to land on deaf ears. After about two and a half months, I once again pleaded my case in my interview with the NKVD representative. He must have believed me this time, or some paper trail proof had arrived because he told me to go when the next transport left and just like that, I was sent back to my unit. I often wondered later if perhaps they had just wanted to get me off their hands after my time of repairing motors and making booze. I concluded that they found out that I was in fact a trained pilot and orders were sent to have me sent back to my squadron immediately.

Then, I received "just another suspended sentence." On the return journey, I had the luxury of squeezing in with the crew of the tractor cab. By this time, they knew that I was, in fact, a fighter pilot, so I was treated with respect. We were all very friendly on the way back, which involved riding on that tractor for over a week, then by military train to Novosibirk in southern Siberia. From there, I reported to another air force outfit, where they made some inquiries on my behalf. Eventually, they found out where I belonged and they issued me a *propiska:* a passport like document with my picture on it that was required to board a train as a valid passenger; you couldn't just buy a ticket and go. One couldn't buy tickets at all; once you were given your destination, they gave you tickets and you got on the train. All along the way, the NKVD kept checking. Officers didn't even ask for the ticket—even though you had to have it—but rather for your *propiska*. If that piece of paper was valid, they didn't bother to match the ticket with the destination.

My unit had been on the move while I was away and it was now closer to the front, closer to Germany. When I reported back to it, my unit was stationed in Kuybyshev. Because I had been away without leave, however, I was sent to court where regardless of my legitimate explanation, I was given another 30-year suspended sentence for being away without permission—and then I learned that I had been selected to be sent away on special training.

CHAPTER 15

Special Training and Staying Alive

Special training involved intense practice in fighting dirty and killing effectively and silently with all sorts of weapons and with my own hands. I was trained in the ancient and secretive Russian hand to hand-fighting technique *Systema Spetsnaz*. This fighting technique was developed centuries ago in Russia by utilizing the best forms from judo, ju-jitsu, savate, boxing, and sambo.

I was taught to resist pain and combat torture, see in the dark, and blend in with any environment so that I could become virtually invisible. Also, they taught me how to acquire information by being like a fly on the wall. Basically, they convert you into a person that you had never been before. My commanders used brainwashing sessions in which they showed me pictures of Germans while playing recorded accounts from people who had gotten out. Through many of the Jewish refugees who had come to Russia from Germany, I had already heard many accounts of Nazi atrocities, including mass murders and picking up Jews as free labour. Although I had heard about those work camps since the beginning of the war, until now I had not known about the extermination camps. At first, people were sent to the camps just to work and death very often resulted. Now I understood what was happening.

The training to withstand pain was what it was—painful: extremely painful. We were subjected to physical pain with a psychologist present. As an example of a session, they put your hand between a door and its frame, and then slowly closed the door on it. This caused slight pain. All the while, the psychologist coaches you to concentrate on another part of your body—your foot, for example. The intensity of the pain increases as the door practically breaks through the skin on your hand. At the same time, you intensify your concentration on your foot. After a while, you focus so much on the foot that you don't really feel the pain in your hand. It's all about the power of concentration; that's the entire answer. At first the trainers put your fingers in the door and press just a bit. By the end, they are pressing so hard that your fingers are bleeding and bruised practically to the bone. By concentrating on your foot, the trainer's nose, or some inanimate object, you eventually don't feel any pain except when you let yourself think about it. Afterwards, you realize that the pain had been excruciating.

It was all about learning how to take yourself out of your body. It took about four to five months of training in order to tolerate that form of torture. Since the enemy would not squeeze fingers and work on a foot simultaneously, this gave us an advantage. The Russians' knowledge about this method of developing introspective, surrogate concentration was considered top secret, and it was closely guarded.

In order to seem invisible, we were taught how to observe other people very carefully in a crowd and then mimic their actions so that we would fit in. If the people are smaller than you, then you stayed away from them. But, even after blending into a crowd, you still had to keep your eyes open and ears sharp. We spent hours training our ears to hear sounds that humans normally do not discern. After a while, I could zero in on a single person whispering in a group. That skill, combined with lip reading, enabled me to understand communication that otherwise would have been beyond comprehension.

We were also trained to see things in the dark. While this method was ineffective in complete darkness, we learned how to see things in surroundings darker than typical nighttime. First, they placed us in a dim chamber where we spent hours upon hours observing and conditioning our eyes by looking at pictures with different shades, shadows, and dimness. The principle was similar to that of learning how to fly into the sun. In a dogfight, the Nazis would always come towards us from the west so that the sun would be directly in our eyes. We had to learn to deal with that, because we didn't have planes equipped with sun visors in the cockpit glass until later when we were flying American planes. Before, when we had no such comfort, we learned to look for the sun's reflection on that plane, like a distortion wave. The trick was to look just to the left or the right of the sun, not at it. Eventually you could make out an aircraft; with practice, it became practically like your regular vision.

And, we learned about "clean killing," as it was called. Many of my missions were designed to find higher-ranking German officers. Sometimes, my orders were to bring them in if I could; if that was impossible for whatever reason, I was to eliminate them, usually with a knife. We were also taught how to use one quick twist of the head to break the neck, which was silent and equally effective.

A typical mission went something like this. We knew where the enemy lines lay, and it would be nighttime. I had to cross into enemy territory—very risky in itself, because I could be hit easily by artillery fire, either by the enemy or even our own gunnery. Mostly, I made my way by crawling and waiting; more crawling and more waiting; and then again. I would move in as close as possible to some population or, occasionally, to enemy headquarters. Once I found my target, I had to wait for the opportune time—which could take several nights. This required extreme patience. Eventually you would get him alone, knock him out, and drag him back through the lines. This part was especially difficult: dragging another man while crawling along; I didn't like the dragging part. I much preferred to just kill the bastards.

It was different with regular soldiers, however. We thought that perhaps some of these guys were just regular folks—but an officer, well, that was different. Most German officers also were party members and were thus contaminated. Many times, I was tempted to simply kill them and just leave them there. Duty came first, however, so I kept dragging them until I fulfilled my mission.

CHAPTER 16

Ambrosia

After the initial German attack, Stalin finally pulled himself out of his cowardly denial and made the commitment to lead his people. He then made his famous broadcast to the nation July 3, 1941. In that speech Stalin paved a pathway for all citizens. During that famous address, Stalin asked his people to "inflict insufferable conditions upon the enemy in occupied areas…to establish partisan units on foot and horseback…bands of saboteurs must be organized to fight hostile detachments, to blow up bridges and roads, to interrupt telephone and telegraph communications, and to set camps and depots on fire.… You must follow him everywhere and annihilate his forces." The partisans, however, were not aided, supported, nor supplied by Stalin's regime until further along in the conflict.

Stalin's appeal may have begun the galvanization of the people, but news of atrocities committed by the Germans fueled the campaign. Men, women, and teenagers were hurrying eagerly to enlist in the partisan movement. Within a few months the faction had grown to include over 100,000 partisan participants engaged behind enemy lines. As a matter of history, 10,000 partisans participated in the Battle of Moscow.

My comrades and I heard stories about heroic acts perpetrated by the partisans and how the combined efforts of those brave souls caused havoc, becoming a constant thorn in the side of the Germans; so much so that special details had to be assigned by the Germans to address the destructive force of the partisans.

Russian partisan in full fighting gear

An 18-year-old member of the Moscow *Komsomol* was caught setting fire to German stables in Petrischevo. Even though she was tortured mercilessly and even while having her left breast cut off, she did not reveal any information. She was later hanged; however, just before her execution she stated: "You can't hang all 190 million of us." Her name was Zoya Kosmodemyanskaya, and her defiance and bravery made her a national heroine and a symbol of partisan resistance. She was posthumously awarded the title "Hero of the Soviet Union" on February 16, 1942.

I was sent on many missions with the Special Forces with orders to rendezvous with partisan units. Mostly, my commands were to deliver radios or dynamite. Sometimes I would lead partisan units on sabotage missions, and in some cases, I was simply sent to assassinate or capture high priority German personnel military targets.

In one particular mission, another Special Forces operative and I were ordered to rendezvous with the partisans, establish a small sabotage team, covertly make it past the front, advance behind enemy lines, and blow up a bridge on one of the main supply routes. As this particular target was well-guarded and the route extremely well-travelled, this mission was carried out with only a small percentage of expected success. As a matter of fact, I was told by my commander, "It's a suicide mission!" My commitment to the mission didn't waver.

Leon (surname unavailable) and I were lying motionless, camouflaged by growth and well-hidden in a ditch just under the bridge. Under the bridge was a bog. Conditions could hardly have been more uncomfortable. We were armed with containers of gasoline, dynamite, and grenades. The stream of German trucks, troops, and materiel on this road seemed endless. The enemy was on high alert and accompanied by dogs. It was pitch dark, yet my special training techniques allowed me to make out in the dimness the cracked lips of my comrade; I realized that I too was in the same condition. We had been at the same spot, hidden in that ditch without any food and little water for over four days and nights. Every centimetre of us was covered by mosquito bites inflicted upon us by the feasting of those ravenous insects.

Our patience paid off! Suddenly, one of the German supply trucks broke down just ahead of the bridge. This produced a gap in the convoy and drew away the attention of several of the foot patrols which had not yet reached the bridge. Like panthers, Leon and I pounced. We drenched the road on the bridge with gallons of gasoline, placed handfuls of explosives and then launched our grenades.

The explosions we heard as we ran meant that our mission was successful; the bridge went up in flames and collapsed. Leon and I split up in order to avoid being captured together. I went north and Leon went south. Within seconds, bright lights were shining in a circular searching manner. I was running full speed and, as I turned my head to look behind me, I saw Leon get hit as machine gun fire raged. I never did find out if Leon survived the mission; it appeared to me that he had been killed. I just kept on fleeing along the edge of the Bug River. Lungs gasping, mouth parched, I stumbled. I ended up with my face buried in mud. It felt cool on my face like thick gooey water. I stuck out my tongue and began lapping like a thirsty dog. "Am I dreaming," I asked myself. No, it was mud. It was a swampy quagmire of insect-infested, moldy mud. I just kept gulping, filling my mouth with that gritty wetness. I couldn't get enough. This is ambrosia! No drink has ever tasted as good.

CHAPTER 17

Captured on a Special Mission

On one particular mission in 1942, I was sent into occupied Russian territory to contact partisans. Naturally, I was disguised as one. I grew a straggly beard and wore a ragged tunic without a belt, using just a rope to hold up my pants. I looked dirty, like a real peasant. Nonetheless, on my way back, I was picked up by two German military police. Perhaps I looked suspicious somehow, or maybe they just wanted to make a point. They took me to a fairly large village where they were part of a larger detachment.

I was taken to the main building and put in a cell in the basement. The dungeon-like cell was small, approximately 2x3 metres and enclosed by steel bars. The door had only a latch and a bolt. And there I was, behind a door tightly latched shut inside a detention cell with a guard armed with a machine gun watching over me. As no officers were present, I assumed they were waiting for one to arrive before interrogating me—or doing whatever they planned to do. It was quite late in the day, so I didn't expect anything to happen before morning.

Meanwhile, I purposely lay against the wall adjacent to the latched door, so the guard wouldn't think that I was up to something. He paced back and forth, looking directly at me every time he turned around to change direction. I just leaned against the wall, waiting patiently, watching that guard go back and forth, and hoping that he would get tired eventually. One small window enabled me to determine that it was getting dark outside. Finally, the guard lit a kerosene lamp. A few hours passed, and I remained motionless, pretending to be asleep. Perhaps curiosity got the best of him, because he reached his arm in and shook me. Perhaps he wanted to know if, indeed, I had fallen asleep. So, I grabbed his hand and twisted it around the bars until his arm snapped. The sound of the fracture was loud but dwarfed by his screams. Although he was screaming with pain, the soldiers upstairs were having fun, engaged in some sort of festivity, thankfully with quite loud music.

Then I unbolted the cell door, grabbed the machine gun from the guard, killed him with it, made my way upstairs, and began shooting immediately. The six of them upstairs were very quickly dead. I grabbed a German coat, put it on over my peasant rags, and made my way out of that building, with the music still blaring behind me. Undetected, I stealthily made it out of town and rendezvoused with a partisan detachment, which provided me with some food and drink.

A few days later I was walking alone along a path when I saw a group of German soldiers approaching. There were six of them. I did what was expected of me...I walked off the path, stood still at the side, bowed my head, and waited for the pack to walk by. As the band of soldiers reached me, I could see that they had been drinking and were all quite intoxicated. One of those bastards grabbed me, pulled out the rope that was being used as a belt for my pants, gave the rope to one of the other soldiers and told the group to tie me up. They complied and wrapped the rope around my waist and tied me to a tree. I was thinking, this predicament isn't very good. How did I manage to let myself get into such a vulnerable position? I knew they intended to kill me!

The bastard that told the others what to do, walked about 20 metres further along the path and the others followed. He drew his machine gun, aimed it directly at me and pulled the trigger. Just as he was about to shoot, I timed it precisely and flumped over pretending that I was shot. As I hung slumped over playing dead, I could hear the bullets hit the tree above my head and felt splinters of tree bark land on my back. The group of soldiers, even more delighted at my apparent demise, was laughing louder and in a state of drunken merriment. Fortunately for me, they did not bother to check on my condition.

I waited motionless, bent over, until I felt it was safe. I then freed myself from the rope and covertly caught up with that group of German soldiers. I followed them until they reached a small cabin. It appeared as if that was where they were going to put up for the upcoming night. I was determined to perpetrate an act of vengeance on the group and especially on the leader who believed he had killed me with his machine gun.

I backtracked along the path and eventually hooked up with a partisan brigade. They recognized me as it was the same bunch who had provided me with clothing, food and shelter earlier. I told them about my experience with that German pack, and it did not take much convincing to enlist a couple of them to assist me in my payback mission. As a matter of fact, I had to turn down most of them because whenever there was an opportunity to kill a few Germans everyone wanted in on it....

By the time the three of us reached the cabin, it was getting dark. We could see the activity of the group through the window. They were eating and drinking. I singled out the position of the bastard who'd shot at me and instructed my two comrades that we would kick in the door and kill the other five of them. I specified that I wanted the leader alive!

It was over in a matter of seconds. The group of German soldiers was not expecting any attack such as the one we committed. Five of them were dead in an instant, and the leader gestured toward some machine guns within his reach. I abruptly aimed my rife at his head while I simply moved my head side to side calmly gesturing "No." I moved my rifle, motioning towards the door. That bastard got the message, and he and I went outside the cabin. I took my time; he didn't die well.

The next day I made my way back to my unit. We had acquired new planes, and I was assigned one: a Vulcan, an American plane that was faster and deadlier than the Messerschmitt!

CHAPTER 18

The Promise

The German bomber attacks continued, but now we had much better planes. I flew often in a Vulcan; however, soon after I fought mostly in the *Yak-1*. The *Yak-1*, just less than nine meters long and three meters high, had a wingspan of 10 meters. This fighter could climb at 1,200 meters per minute and had a range of over 850 kilometers. Its maximum speed was 600 km/h. The *Yak-1* became my favorite plane. I found it exhilarating to fire the 20 mm *ShVAK* cannon that shot through the propeller hub. It also was equipped with two 7.62mm machine guns (each with 375 rounds) for targets on the ground. All guns were controlled by the stick and could be fired easily with one hand. Sometimes I flew in a *LaGG-3*, which had a wooden body and could fly over 625 km/h, but it did not perform nearly as well as the *Yak-1*.

The Yakovlev Yak-1 *a maneuverable, fast, and competitive Russian fighter aircraft*

These better planes gave all the Russian pilots a new and invigorating sense of confidence. Finally, we had an equal chance with the enemy. Often, I would spend time between squadron runs flying solo, bombing German targets just to cause as much havoc as possible. I was strongly motivated to kill as many of the enemy as I could.

One time, when I was fighting alongside other Soviet squadrons, we managed to divert some German bombers. Another squadron then took over, chasing the bombers while we circled around trying to take down the Messerschmitts that were protecting them.

Suddenly, I was hit. I didn't see it coming, but some vital part was shot up because the plane started to burn. Thankfully, I was close to our air base, so I headed towards it. The damaged Yak was extremely difficult to control. Not only had the engine cut out and caught fire (persuading me that I might blow up any second), but the tail was a mess, too. The wheels had locked, so I couldn't put them down for landing. Despite my lack of control, I somehow planed it down, landed on the belly of the aircraft, and skidded about 100 meters or so to a stop. When I then tried to undo my safety belt, it was stuck!

As a result of the way I had landed, the plane was badly broken and tilting to the left. I kept trying desperately to release the seatbelt, but it just wouldn't give. Expecting the plane to explode at any second, I reached urgently for the knife in my left back pocket. It was no use; I was too jammed in to access my knife despite the adrenalin rush of my life-or-death struggle. The heat of the fire was intensifying rapidly, and I remember thinking, "Well, Joe, this is it. You're done. This time there's no way out, and you're going to die right here." It seemed inevitable that I would be blown to bits—which brought some comfort that death would be quick, preferable to burning slowly to death. In a way, we were always ready to die. Each time we went up, we felt the possibility that we wouldn't come back alive lingering in the back of our minds. But I never felt afraid of dying; I believe that I was born without the "fear gene." I do not remember a single time when I actually felt afraid.

Unexpectedly, I saw Sergei Kargopolski; I had seen him around but didn't really know him. He was one of the mechanics, and I saw from the corner of my eye that he was running towards me. Apparently, he had seen me coming down and hurried over to help me. I hoped that he would be able to rescue me in time. Fortunately for me, he had come with a knife. After just a couple of hacks, Sergei cut me out of the harness straps, pulled me out of the cockpit, dragged me about 15 meters from the flames, and pushed me flat on the ground. My willing body aided him, as experience had taught both of us to be as close to the ground and as flat as possible when a plane exploded. You did not want to be standing upright near an exploding airplane. We lay there, waiting for the plane to blow, and a few seconds later…kaboom!

After that incident, our friendship grew. Sergei was an easy-going man with a face you could trust. Like me, he was not very keen on the Russian way of things. He wasn't outwardly defiant against Stalin's regime, as that would have meant being shot, but he spoke somewhat openly to me about some of things he disliked about the communist system and life in Russia. I could tell by how he talked that he was not dedicated to the Soviets. He mentioned that Russian authorities had killed his family during the revolution. At the front, with people dying all around, people spoke more freely—but carefully, as a single insult towards Stalin could mean instant execution if overheard by the wrong person.

Sergei was one of the few men to whom I revealed that I had been born in Poland. As the Russian and Polish languages were so closely related, I spoke Russian without a detectable accent. Consequently, people assumed that I was a Russian, born and raised as a comrade just like them. I told Sergei that I wanted to go back home to Poland after the war ended. He told me about his two daughters, one in Alma-Ata and the other in Moscow. Perhaps he hated Russia more than he said, because he confided in me that his biggest dream was for his daughters to live in freedom outside of Russia. Although he had lost contact with his older daughter, he knew where Sophie, the younger one, was. He asked me to promise that, if I ever became able to leave Russia, I would take Sophie with me. I made him that promise, not only because he had saved my life, but because I felt it was something that I just had to do. Later, I would go to Alma-Ata and introduce myself to Sophie, bringing with me the letter and picture her father had provided me. I would find out what she thought about her father's wishes and the promise I had made to him.

CHAPTER 19

Cigarettes Can Save your Life

Every now and then, fighter pilots were granted two or three-day rest periods. During one particular rest period, four fellow pilots and I set up kind of a campsite in the woods about one kilometre from the airfield. We were still on the defensive in the war and were stationed quite a way from Kharkov at the time when it was being bombed rather heavily.

It was the middle of the summer, and we found a *polanka* or small clearing in the woods, pitched a tent, and built a fire-pit. There we played music, told stories, read, cooked, drank vodka, smoked cigarettes, and just relaxed. It was always great to indulge in this recuperative experience—a rare refuge from the war.

Attracted by its bawling one afternoon, the five of us came upon a calf in the field near our camp. The calf was thin, limping and bleeding from a deep gash in one leg. We looked at each other and, as if by telepathy, I raised my gun and fired. I shot the calf directly in the head and it died instantly. Somehow, we were going to find a way to cook and eat that veal. We were certainly not going to let this rare luxury of fresh meat go by the wayside.

I remembered that there was a deserted house on a ridge just about a kilometre away. The house walls were caved in and the residence was devoid of any furniture or household items; however, I did recollect that there was a four-legged bathtub in the bathroom of that abandoned abode.

We left one of my comrades to gather wood for a fire and the rest of us ascended to that decrepit house and, with vigor and enthusiastic anticipation, we carried that bathtub from its place in the bathroom to the field. Many trips were made to the creek in order to fill our canteens with water, which was then poured into the tub. We kept this up until the water level in the tub was up to about halfway. We always carried a knife with us. While the fire burned and the water began to boil, we all carved away at the calf. In time the tub was filled with the most edible pieces of the young bovine.

We sat and stared at the tub, waiting patiently and licking our chops in anticipation of freshly boiled veal. As the heavenly aroma began to permeate our olfactory senses, we regaled ourselves with stories of our favorite and most fabulous meals. By now, we were practically salivating and our eagerness to begin the feast was at its highest peak.

"Shit! Enemy plane!" I yelled out. "Dive for cover!" There was no time to grab any of those calf pieces and one of the damn bombs was a direct hit on our makeshift pot. That bloody bomb smashed the tub and the calf to smithereens. Bye-bye beef. We collected what we could and moved campsites.

Every morning, the other pilots took turns walking to the airfield to pick up the daily supplies. It was their job, not mine, because I had a higher rank. One day we were in the tent at mid-morning, all taking advantage of the leave by sleeping in. As we were waking up, one of my comrades—the one whose turn it was to go on the ration run—began complaining that he was still tired and wanted to get a little more sleep. I had a craving for a cigarette; we were out of them and I felt like walking, so I volunteered to go. I quickly got up, dressed, and made my way out of the tent. After relieving myself in the nearby bushes, I began strolling towards the airfield, whistling as I went.

Just beyond the woods, I heard some unusual sounds. I looked up and saw that a German light bomber had been shot at and damaged, and it was flying away towards the front. I didn't know why that German plane was alone. I thought maybe the pilot was on reconnaissance or had gotten separated from his squadron. In any event, the plane was emitting black smoke and I watched as the pilot released his bombs. I could tell that he wasn't aiming at any targets, but only lightening his load in order to acquire more velocity for his escape.

One of the bombs fell and exploded in the exact area of the clearing where my comrades were still sleeping. I turned around and began to jog towards them. Back at the campsite, I witnessed a hole in the ground and pieces of my comrades scattered about; they had been blown to bits. I wondered if they had heard the whistle of the bomb at the same time as I was whistling. When a bomb is released at that height directly over your head, by the time you hear its whistle, it's too late. To this day I don't think that German bomber pilot ever knew that he had killed those guys. I had not experienced any sort of premonition of danger or any feeling that I just had to get out of there. Nothing like that; I just wanted a smoke. Fortunately for me, that craving for a cigarette saved my life.

CHAPTER 20

"Not One Step Back"

By mid-1942, the German invasion had already cost Russia more than 6 million soldiers. Half had been killed and half captured. Germany had managed to secure a large part of Russia's vast territory and many of her resources. Because of the arctic winter, however, exhausted German troops halted their assault just before reaching Moscow. In fact, Russian forces had managed to push the Germans back a little.

In the summer of 1942, when Russia was still very weak from its tremendous losses, the German military was again ready to demonstrate its formidable fighting force. Hitler's generals wanted to attack in the direction of Moscow again, in order to take Russia's capital city—its heart and nerve center—and to crush most of Russia's remaining military forces while doing so.

Hitler, on the other hand, was listening less and less to his generals. Instead, in April he had issued *War Directive 41*, which detailed his plan for the Russian Front for the summer of 1942, code named *Operation Blue*. This plan would concentrate all available forces on the southern flank of the long front, destroy the front-line Russian forces there, and then advance in two directions to the primary and secondary objectives— the two most important remaining industrial centers in South Russia. The primary objective, involving an advance far southeast and through the mountainous Caucasus region, was to capture the rich oil fields on the Caspian Sea. The secondary objective involved an advance east to Stalingrad, a major industrial and transportation center on the west bank of the wide Volga River. This river was the main waterway of inner Russia, running all the way from north of Moscow to the Caspian Sea in the south.

The final objective was to reach Stalingrad itself and bombard it with heavy artillery until it could no longer sustain itself as an industrial or transportation center. The German army achieved this objective with minimal losses on the first day of the Battle of Stalingrad. But the Germans' stubborn battle to occupy the city itself eventually caused their defeat at Stalingrad—combined with Hitler's later refusal to retreat from the city. These actions would cost Hitler his entire southern campaign. Both sides, however, suffered tremendous losses. Once Hitler's forces had entered the city named after the Soviet dictator Stalin, Hitler's arch enemy, Hitler became so obsessed with occupying Stalingrad that the large German force in and near Stalingrad was eventually destroyed to the last man.

The German attack in southern Russia began June 28, 1942, just over a year after its invasion of Russia had begun. The Germans advanced rapidly in a Blitzkrieg of armour and air power, and were followed by their Italian, Romanian, and Hungarian allies, whose task was to secure the long German flanks. The Russian Front collapsed, and the Germans rapidly advanced towards the Volga River, south Russia's last natural line of defense.

On July 27, 1942, in a desperate attempt to stop the collapse, Stalin issued *Ni Shagu Nazad*, or "Not One Step Back" (also called *General Order 227*) that said "every granule of Soviet soil must be stubbornly defended to the last drop of blood." NKVD units, partisans, nationalists, and even convicted prisoners were placed behind the Russian Front units. Called "blocking detachments," they were given orders to kill anyone who attempted to desert or retreat. *General Order 227* appealed to Russian patriotism, clarifying just how severe the situation was, and thus galvanized the entire Russian forces.

Despite their effort, the Russian 62nd and 64th armies west of Stalingrad failed to stop the advancing Germans. The empty, arid prairie provided good terrain for easy attack, and the Germans pushed the Russians back towards the city's urban stretch along the Volga's west bank.

By August 23, 1942, the spearhead of the German 6th Army reached the Volga just north of Stalingrad and captured an eight-kilometre-wide strip along its bank. German tanks and artillery began to sink crossing ships and ferries. On that day, other units of the 6th army reached the outskirts of Stalingrad, followed by hundreds of bombers and dive-bombers of the Luftwaffe's 4th air fleet. The pilots began a heavy bombardment that would continue for five days and nights, destroying or damaging every building in the city.

CHAPTER 21

The Kitten of the Volga

By late August of 1942, my unit was stationed approximately 50 kilometers east of Stalingrad. By then, the Russian Central Command had lost contact with a major brigade of about 800 tanks that was supposed to have been settled in and camouflaged, awaiting the onset of the German attack on Stalingrad.

General Vasily Petrenko, officer of the Russian Tank Planning Division, called me in and asked me to volunteer for a special mission. He asked me to fly an unmarked plane and find the exact location of that misplaced tank brigade (if in fact it was still there) and deliver a radio to them. Central Command needed to establish ongoing communication with that tank division. The commanders knew that they could not send anybody on foot or by jeep, because German soldiers already had infiltrated the area between the Russian tank brigade and Stalingrad.

Flying high above the Don River to avoid German detection, I was about 100 kilometres from Stalingrad, when I saw a concentration of at least four German tank divisions—though it was hard to estimate the exact number through my binoculars. Transport trains were moving on two tracks toward the tanks. I could imagine them hauling food, supplies, cannons, and other armaments. This huge massing of military hardware meant only one thing—confirmation of an inevitable and imminent attack on Stalingrad.

I was flying in an unmarked biplane to avoid recognition from any German fighters doing reconnaissance. Having been provided with the general location of the Russian tank brigade, I would be able to spot it even though it was camouflaged, because I knew its general whereabouts. When I finally located the Russian brigade, I sought out a field nearby with the intention of landing. As I began my descent, ground troops began firing at me, but I made it down in one piece nevertheless.

The importance of my mission became apparent when a jeep appeared with a couple of military police, and I presented to them my documents along with the radio. The MPs then brought me in front of General Vasily Chuikov, who was very glad to have contact again with Central Command. I produced a sealed letter that I was asked to hand deliver to him; he accepted it, and I was dismissed.

My mission accomplished, I headed back towards my plane—but before I could reach it, a German fighter pilot blasted it and rendered it inoperable. Maybe the German did it just for fun or perhaps he thought that my unmarked Polikarpov belonged to some Russian officer or dignitary. Even though some of my enemy's actions actually could be justified, I felt angry nonetheless.

My comrades couldn't send me back because there were German lines crossing in that direction. They did provide me with a ride, however, to within 40 kilometres south of Stalingrad. That's as far as they dared to go. I was once again on my own.

I took compass bearings and began walking, mostly at night and hiding during the day. In a few days, I had managed to reach, an abandoned village about 10 kilometers south of Stalingrad. It was completely deserted as residents had previously been evacuated for fear of impending German advances that would have gone right through their homes.

A few months earlier, the German armies had suffered an ignominious defeat outside Moscow. The result was that Hitler was now obsessed with Stalingrad and determined to launch a major offensive on Russia as soon as the ground was firm enough for his Panzer tank divisions to roll. Stalin, on the other hand, was equally determined to keep the city bearing his name from falling into enemy hands. Stalingrad would be defended at any cost. Some 500,000 Russians would die, obeying Stalin's order of "not one step back."

Hitler's plan was that German Army Group North would take Stalingrad, the Central Front was to hold, and the south would be the main theatre for the summer campaign to break through to the Volga and the Caucasus.

The Germans were always seeking oil because the entire war was being waged using combustion engines. The Third Reich depended on synthetic production of what came out of the large Romanian and Hungarian fields. At this time, the Caucasus produced about three quarters of Russia's oil and also had vast resources of iron ore and some coal. The logic was simple and the goal crucial. If Germany could deprive the Soviets of fuel, Hitler thought he could bring Russia to her knees.

Hitler ordered simultaneous attacks on the Caucasus and Stalingrad against the protests of many German officers. To their dismay, the engagement moved forward. Despite German advances, the Red Army lost far fewer men than before. Stalin had learned that it was far better to retreat his armies as the Germans moved forward rather than risk the slaughter of men and the devastation of armaments.

Hitler changed tactics again and ordered the 4th Panzer division, which had been heading towards the Caucasus, to swing around and join the 6th Army in an attack on Stalingrad. Simultaneously, he ordered the detachment of a considerable portion of the artillery that had been heading towards the Caucasus and sent those up towards Stalingrad.

The German army was facing an ever-weakening Stalingrad. By August 23, Colonel General Friederich Paulus and his 6th Army were on the left bank of the Volga north of Stalingrad and advancing into the suburbs. That day every German plane available bombed Stalingrad. The five-day attack involved on average more than 1,000 sorties per day, which killed 40,000 civilians and wounded 150,000 more.

I was still in the village, south of Stalingrad, when the bombing started. Seeking safe shelter, I eventually crawled into a hole in the basement of an abandoned house and hid out there. From that fissure a lone witness as Stalingrad suffered through five days of bombing.

Stalingrad was a highly industrialized city of 445,000 people that stretched 20 kilometres from south to north on either side of the Volga River. The weather was hot and sticky. The city's north end was home to the largest tank and tractor factory in the world, the Molotov Factory, which employed more than 20,000 men and women. Piers, storage sheds, and the loading docks of four ports snaked along both sides of the river.

The area was bustling 24 hours a day with heavy barges and traffic of all kinds—all rushing industrial resources from throughout Russia to fill the ever-hungry maw of the great city that was the guardian of and gateway to Russia.

If Stalingrad fell, the whole of Russia would be wide open to the Germans with all her resources and endless space. What a strategic victory it would have been for Hitler to occupy Stalingrad, the very namesake of Russia's supreme commander.

On August 23, 1942, the Battle of Stalingrad officially began. First the noise came: thundering and endless. From my position in the abandoned house, I saw wave after wave of planes bearing down on Stalingrad—hundreds of planes per wave looking like huge flocks of blackbirds. When the leading wave dropped its load of bombs, I could hear the ear-piercing whistles as they fell. While one wave sheared off, another took its place. The sky was black, and the number of enemy aircraft seemed incessant, infinite in fact. The destruction that followed was final and devastating. Just how many planes ripped the air above me was impossible to estimate. For five days and four nights in that basement shelter, I witnessed the systematic and terrible obliteration of Stalingrad. All her history, and all her industry, power and might were eradicated. At night German planes dropped incendiary bombs, burning what had been turned into skeleton and ash by the daytime raids. Later, it was said that the flames were so intense that they provided enough illumination for someone to read a newspaper at night up to 60 kilometers away.

Five days later, in the afternoon, it suddenly became quiet, as if existence itself had been utterly destroyed. You could hear a grain of sand fall. The stillness hurt my ears. Every 15 or 20 minutes, the engine of a German scout plane broke the silence. Occasionally, a German bomber buzzed overhead, dropping bombs at targets on the river. Otherwise, it seemed as if the world had died; it was eerie. I wondered if I had landed on another planet. Nothing stirred—not a leaf, beast, nor bird. Not even a whisper of air fanned my face. "Am I truly the only one left alive?" I asked God.

As I started walking towards the banks of the Volga, I saw a sea of belongings: bedding, furniture, kitchen appliances, food, and clothing. Everything to keep body and soul together was strewn just where people had fallen; thousands and thousands of panicking refugees desperately tried to cross the river ahead of the bombs. Finally, I scrambled to the edge of the Volga, a river in flames. Streams of gasoline, diesel fuel, and chemicals burned, punctuated by channels of clear water; and I had no choice except somehow to find a path across the river.

The haunting silence continued. No rustling or earth sounds did I hear; no one breathed or even stirred. Not even my own inhalation could break the hush. Once again, but intermittently, I heard the puttering engine noise of a German spotter that proved to me that sound still existed.

Then I heard it; an infinitesimally tiny noise. I looked around, my trained ears straining eagerly for the source. A kitchen cupboard stood open on the ground nearby, with all its contents spilling out. Leaning against it was the portrait of an elderly woman inside a frame made of rice and painted gold. With silken grey hair piled regally upon the top of her head, her countenance was kind, proud, and wise. In front of that, staring fixedly at her features and meowing weakly, was the tiniest black and white kitten I had ever seen. I just stood there bewildered. Staring at that helpless animal affirmed the existence of another life; I was astonished for a few moments. Somehow the sight of this small living creature, so completely vulnerable before the overwhelming supremacy of war, summed up all the horror and futility of what I had witnessed and to which, by duty, I was bound to return.

Rummaging through the debris, I eventually found a can of sardines and opened it with my knife, eating some myself and leaving the spoils for the ravenous black and white kitten. Wishing it well, I was now able to concentrate on my own survival.

I took two sideboards from a wooden bed and tied them to my chest with makeshift ropes that I fashioned from a sheet. I eased my way into the river and was pleased to see that the boards helped me stay buoyant. I paddled my way with my hands through the channels between the flames of burning oil and debris. At times the openings narrowed, and I felt certain that I would be burned alive. It must have taken me about three harrowing hours to cross the river in this manner.

By sunset, I was able to shed those blessed boards and walk wearily eastwards, guided by the stars. I slept in an abandoned house in the first small hamlet I came across. The village seemed deserted by everyone but the man in the moon, who peeked timidly at me through the window as if he had never seen a human being before.

Next morning, immediately after sunup, I continued eastward on the road out of town until I met up with members of a Russian military patrol, who took me back to my unit to report what I had seen. Two days later, the Battle for Stalingrad began in earnest. Germans and Russians killed each other, back and forth like lethal dancers, street by street, house by house, hole by hole and eyeball to eyeball in the relentless war of attrition called by the Germans "Rattenkrieg" (War of the Rats).

It took the Germans just months to invade Russia and reach Stalingrad—such were the technological advantages. It took years of Russian blood, guts, and determination to root them out.

In November of 1942, Stalin sent hundreds of thousands of fresh Russian troops trained in Siberia to take the region. From the east, they arrived on skis camouflaged in white outerwear and boots—making this massive army silent and invisible. Including these invigorated troops; Marshal Georgy Konstantinovich Zhukov used six armies of 1 million men to envelope the city. The fifth tank regiment led by Prokofy Romanenko attacked from the north, as did the 21st Army led by Ivan Chistyakov, the 65th Army led by Pavel Batov, and the 24th Army led by Ivan Galinin. The 64th, 57th, and 521st armies attacked from the south. The attacking armies met up on November 23 to the west of Stalingrad.

This colossal force surrounded the Germans and opened up with machine gun fire, which created chaos and panic. Concurrently, artillery was brought in and the Russian-designed Katyusha multiple rocket launchers were also deployed into action. Subsequently, the Russian Air Force attacked. This combination caused the complete and utter decimation of the German forces surrounding Stalingrad.

On January 31, 1943, Hitler promoted Colonel General Friedirch Paulus to Field Marshal *in absentia*, expecting this to bring him back to Berlin under his influence. Paulus and his staff were surrounded in their headquarters in the basement of the Univermag Department Store. To date, no German field marshal had been captured alive. This promotion was as good as an order to commit suicide. Instead, Field Marshal Paulus surrendered to his captor, Lieutenant Fyodor Mikhailovich Yelchenko, that very day.

On February 2, the remaining German army (including 91,000 soldiers and 24 generals) capitulated. These prisoners, in conjunction with many others, were later put to work rebuilding Stalingrad and other Russian cities. When all was said and done, Stalingrad became the graveyard for more than 400,000 German soldiers and over 1 million Soviets. Field Marshal Paulus remained in Russia after the war and became a professor teaching at the Moscow Military Academy.

What an unpredictable world! To my dying day, I will always remember vividly the black and white kitten meowing forlornly at the portrait of that woman. For one brief moment on centre stage in the theatre of the desolation of war, entire existence came down to the two us: that tiny kitten of the Volga and me.

CHAPTER 22

Sophie

Having received some time off, I decided it was time to meet Sophie. Armed with the letter and pictures from her father, I headed to Alma-Ata, located in southeastern Kazakhstan, and far from the front lines. It was a long and arduous trip, mostly by train, and when I arrived, I had no definite information to help me in locating her. Eventually I found her working as a nurse in an army hospital. Sophie was looking after the soldiers who would not be going back for duty; they were the severely wounded, the amputees, and the mentally destroyed.

Though I had seen pictures of her and had had no romantic intentions toward her, I could not ignore her breathtaking beauty when I saw her in person. Her long, flaming red hair flowed like ocean waves around a gorgeous countenance, and she boasted the figure of a pin-up girl. Her eyes possessed a classic seductive sparkle, and when she spoke, any man's heartbeat would race. In many ways Sophie reminded me of Rita Hayworth.

Joseph's future wife Sophie

Sophie had never heard of me, but I introduced myself to her as a friend of her father and gave her the letter and pictures. We shared stories, and I updated her about what was going on at the front. I recounted how her father had saved my life and the promise I had made to him. Sophie became very excited when she heard about her father's wish that, if I were to leave Russia, I would take her with me. She was more than willing to leave and actually possessed a strong desire to get out of Russia. Her upbringing had taught her to mistrust the whole regime. Sophie's family had some history with the communists. She told me that the Bolshevists had killed her grandparents and had shot her uncle after the revolution because he was a "white officer" in the Czar's army. Her mother's remorse and bitterness about this had aided in her untimely death as well.

For two days we hung out, getting to know each other and sharing some laughs. This time, for me, was a small oasis of calm amidst the constant tenseness caused by the war. When it was time for me to say goodbye, I told her that I would be back someday when the war ended.

It would not be until quite some time after the end of the war that it would suddenly dawn on me, like a sledge-hammer striking a railway spike, that "a promise is a promise," and I would have to risk my life in order to go back for Sophie and honour the promise I had made to her father.

CHAPTER 23

Kursk

We felt it coming. After Stalingrad, the Red Army launched a massive offensive. By April 1943, the Germans had been driven back some 1,000 kilometres. In response, the German High Command sent troops from Western Europe to the Eastern Front. There were now more German divisions in Russia than at any other time during the war.

The Germans shortened the front, regrouped with their new forces, and managed to hold their ground temporarily. The Red Army had taken Kharkov and then lost it again. Zhukov recaptured Voronezh, and farther north, Soviet forces managed to create a salient 240 kilometers long and 160 kilometers wide near the town of Kursk. Even with their reinforcements, the German armies were incapable of advancing anywhere along that line. They planned an offensive called *Operation Citadel* that concentrated 50 divisions on the flanks of the Soviet salient. Their goal: to exact revenge for the Stalingrad humiliation.

In late June, under Zhukov's command, I was directed to fly continuous reconnaissance missions west of the front, looking particularly for enemy tank divisions. The Germans moved their tanks at night and camouflaged them during the day. I had been well trained, however, and knew what to look for. When I saw a large forested area with a clearing—bent trees and foliage flattened—I knew that this indicated a potential site for a previously camouflaged tank division. About a week before the battle, which began July 5, I spotted a lot of enemy tank movements. I reported back immediately what I had seen, providing another piece in the defences of the Russian high command.

Before the end of June, 900,000 German soldiers with 10,000 pieces of artillery, 2,700 tanks, and 2,000 aircraft were facing the Russians. It had been predictable that the Germans would attack the Kursk salient; the generals of the Third Reich had built their entire success on this pincer movement. The *Stavka* (the Moscow High Command), however, had received detailed intelligence of the enemy plans through a stream of reports from a Russian spy in the German high command and additional information from the British breaking of the Enigma code machines. And, a day before the attack, a German prisoner provided the Red Army with the precise time of the eminent attack. We were ready.

Zhukov was in command of the entire operation. His plan, *Operation Kutuzov*, was to allow the Germans to exhaust themselves and then launch a massive counterattack. Russian troops of the Central and Voronezh Fronts consisted of 1.3 million men, up to 20,000 guns, 3,444 tanks, and 2,172 planes under the command of generals Konstantin Rokossovsky and Nikolai Vatutin. They were to absorb and repel the initial attack. To the rear, General Ivan Konev's reserve at the Steppe Front would wait with the infantry, tank, and motorized divisions to deliver the decisive blow. Since May the Red Army and about 300,000 civilians had been hard at work laying about 400,000 mines and digging approximately 1,000 trenches. The civilians had repaired almost 3,000 kilometers of roads. In some places, the defenses were up to 45 kilometres deep.

In the early morning of July 5, we started to hear noise. We soon found out that the Soviet high command had prior knowledge of the impending attack and, to destroy morale, it had orchestrated massive artillery bombardments on the German positions.

By the time we were ordered into the air to provide support, Russian and German tanks were already engaged and so close to each other that we could not risk taking out a German tank without crippling one of our own. Some of my comrades and I first engaged some of the German *Junkers JU 87 Stuka* bombers. We managed to shoot down a few and forced many others to scatter. Then, I took the initiative and flew west of the battle; some of my comrades followed. Now we were positioned so that we could view Germans tanks moving into the skirmishes. They were isolated enough that we could take them out by discharging our anti-tank rockets. Although many German fighter planes had been protecting the tanks, we somehow managed to break through. We rendered many German tanks useless before we had to turn back for refueling, but I'll never know exactly how many.

By the time we took off again and headed over the battlefield, we couldn't tell what was what. Basically, I was flying over black clouds of dust, smoke, burning tanks, and exploding landmines. Occasionally, a German plane would appear, and we took it on—but that was just about the only other contribution we could make to the battle. We couldn't identify which tanks were which but had to try to keep German planes from flying over to our side and damaging our tanks. We shot down more than 200 German planes.

The Germans had performed exactly as Zhukov had predicted. Both sides engaged in what was to be the fiercest tank fight in history. The Russians executed two counterattacks. Their counter-offensive on the Orel salient, to the north of the Kursk bulge, was so successful that the Germans were forced to withdraw; on August 23, Hitler called off the attack. He failed to appreciate our improved air force and underestimated the Soviet defences around Kursk; therefore, Germany lost the Battle of Kursk.

A few days after the conflict, to allay my curiosity, I flew towards the battlefield, landed close to the site of the catastrophe, and ventured through the aftermath. It was like a graveyard of tanks, both Russian and German. I witnessed the remains of thousands of tanks in all states of destruction—many burnt; many blown apart; many in pieces; and many still burning. Thousands of soldiers from both sides lay dead, burned, unconscious, or blown to pieces. "What a bloody mess!" I thought to myself.

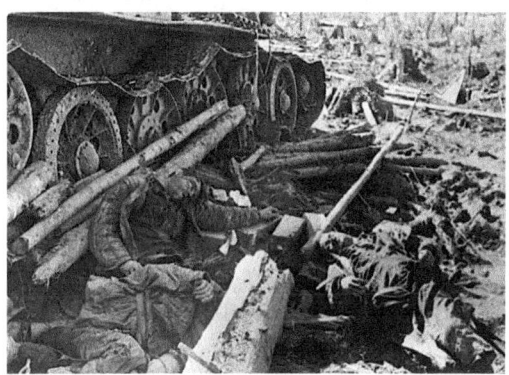

Grizzly aftermath of Kursk

CHAPTER 24

Fake It Till You Make It

One day in mid-December 1943, I was stationed near the Western Front when I was told to report to the commanding general. I was escorted into the general's office, I saluted him and stood at attention. Beside me to my left, stood an elderly gentleman dressed in a fine suit. The general commanded, "At ease." I relaxed my standing posture while placing my arms behind my back. He had my file opened in his hands.

As he closed my file he spoke, "Captain Halpern, it seems that you studied music in gymnasium." I answered, "Yes, sir." The general continued, "That's excellent because I'm assigning you to the entertainment committee." He said casually, "You are now the conductor for the Russian Air Force Orchestra." He paused for a second then added, "Congratulations." I answered with exaggerated pride, "I will fulfill this duty with honour, sir!" As the words came out of my mouth, I was wondering to myself: "How the hell am I going to pull this off?" He pointed to the gentlemen standing beside me, "This is your tailor: he will take your measurements." The general then stood up, handed me a black briefcase and a black circular tubed container; the container was about 50 centimetres long and three centimetres in diameter. "These are for you." The general then called for his aide. The tailor and I waited in silence until the aide arrived. Then the general spoke, "He will tell you what to do." Referring to the aide, "You leave for the east in one week. You are dismissed."

The tailor, the general's aide, and I left the general's office to an adjacent room. I carried the briefcase and black tube. The tailor asked me to undress and then began taking my measurements, assisted by the general's aide; he even measured my feet. When finished measuring me, the tailor left. The aide then said to me, "I need you back here tomorrow at 1300 hours."

At first opportunity of being alone, I took a moment to examine the contents of the briefcase and the black tube. I had a feeling that the tube might contain a conductor's baton; "Yup," I murmured to myself as I slid the baton out of the tube. I was overwhelmed by how light this finely crafted, smooth as silk wooden baton was. I tried gesticulating several maestro-like motions with it. Inside the briefcase were a repertoire list, a list of the orchestra musicians including what instrument they played, and conductor scores of musical arrangements. While glancing briefly through each piece (about 30 of them), I was relieved to see that none had complicated time signatures. I had previously played the accordion, reading music only in the bass and treble clefs. When observing percussion notation, and music for each section both in the alto and tenor clefs, I muttered, "Fake it till you make it."

After arriving back at my quarters and having a bite to eat, I spent the entire evening and night going over each musical piece. I didn't feel any fear, anxiety or dread about fulfilling this duty; I was just hoping that I would be able to pull this off and do a good job.

The next day, I reported to the general's aide. He offered me some coffee, which I eagerly accepted. A few moments later, the tailor arrived with a couple of suit bags and a suitcase. In the suit bags were a tuxedo and a black suit. The briefcase was filled with shirts, ties, bow ties, socks, a pair of black dress shoes, and accessories like cufflinks, tie clips, and pocket squares. I tried on the clothes; all were a perfect fit and pictures were taken. "These are for your promotional materials," the aide said, as I began to start feeling, well quite frankly, like a star. I always felt a certain amount of pride in my accomplishments and likewise appreciated recognition. I did not, however, seek adoration and avoided being in the spotlight.

Later in the day, I returned to my barracks, dropped of the clothing and suitcase, wrote down all the titles of the pieces (including the names of the composers), picked up the baton case in my hand, and tucked the body of it between my arm and my ribs like a high-ranking officer. I had a bite to eat and made my way to the library. I researched books on conducting and spent the next few days at the library listening to the pieces. Thankfully, the library had recordings of most of the them on 78 RPM vinyl discs; I spent many hours in the library with headphones on my ears, with the baton in my hand, practicing the movements of my body imitating a conductor, while listening to and memorizing the pieces. I wondered if it would be possible to omit from actual performances some of the pieces that I could not find a recording of and did not know how they went. I figured that while rehearsing with the orchestra I would play it by ear. I was quite surprised that all were jazz pieces: not one classical title among them.

Jazz was first introduced to Russia on October 1, 1922, when the premiere jazz concert was held in Moscow by amateur musicians. It's hard to believe that the Soviet leadership allowed this as appreciation for jazz and other popular music grew. Initially the leadership viewed jazz as the music of the oppressed Afro-American minority and could well be used as another instrument in the political struggle. Regardless, soon American jazz bands the like of Frank Witers and Sam Wooding visited the Soviet Union performing series of concerts with immense success. I was introduced to American jazz watching the movie "Sun Valley Serenade" just before getting rounded up and sent to the dolomite mine. It featured Glenn Miller; the most popular pieces I could remember were "I Know Why", "Chattanooga Choo Choo," and of course many Soviets could hum out the melody of "In the Mood." The communist party considered jazz *foreign bourgeoisie* and for the proletariat.

The train ride to the east took a few days. I used this time efficiently; with a gift of a few rubles, one of the stewards procured me a small mirror, so I could watch myself going over the pieces while perfecting my newly-acquired conductor's skills. I was gaining confidence and was especially enjoying the beginning and ending gestures.

Arriving in Kazakhstan, I was driven to a military base. Shortly after, the first rehearsal was scheduled, at which I was introduced to the members of the orchestra. The level of respect they showed for me was remarkable. After all, none had any clue about who I was or what experience I had or what authority I commanded. It was a 24-piece orchestra including drums, stand-up bass, trombones, trumpets, saxes, strings, and a piano. As mentioned, I previously had a list of musicians and had studied their names; it did not take long for all of us to be comfortable with one another.

The rehearsal went surprisingly very well, during which I only made comments like "That sounded great." or "Let's try it again with a little more feeling." I asked questions and for suggestions on tempo, especially with the pieces I was unfamiliar with. When all was said and done, we managed to get through the entire repertoire sounding great; no pieces needed to be omitted and the musicians, I felt, could not tell that this was my first time doing this. After rehearsals, I was always the last to leave and while putting my baton back in its case, like a reoccurring theme, each time I murmured…you guessed it—"Fake it till you make it."

The Russian Air Force Orchestra toured eastern Europe for a couple of months, performing mostly two-nighters on Fridays and Saturdays. Occasionally we played a matinee and every now again we performed on a weekday night. The highlight for me was when we performed for two nights at the Uyghur Theatre in Kazakhstan. The privilege to perform at the Uyghur Theatre meant worthiness of the highest musical professionalism. It was kind of like the Carnegie Hall of Russia. It was the first professional theatre in the history of the Uyghur people of Kazakhstan, opened in 1934 with the musical drama "Anarkhan" by D. Asimov and A. Sadyrov. The Uyghur Theatre was formed during the most severely repressive period of the Soviet Stalin era. From 1941 to 1961, the theatre was relocated to the Alma-Ata region and, during the war, the Uyghur Theatre lived mostly on wheels. It served four large areas: Enbekshi-Kazakh, Chlik, Uygur, and Dzharkent.

One day my services as the conductor were abruptly terminated and just like that, I found my way on a train back to the Western Front. Of all the experiences in my life, few could compare the intense sensations of jubilation and immense overwhelming spiritual and psycho-physiological gratification one feels while conducting a well-polished and accomplished orchestra. I now know first-hand, why orchestra conductors experience one of the highest longevity rates.

Joseph Halpern formally dressed for his debut as a conductor

Joseph Halpern by poster for the jazz concert at the Uyghur Theatre

CHAPTER 25

It's Over

By May 1944, most of the cities having been bombed, our squadrons were camped mostly in the fields where we erected mobile stations. We camouflaged our Yaks when the planes were not involved in a conflict, with tree branches, leaves, and bushes.

One summer day, the alarm sounded, and I took off with a couple of squadrons to engage in the inevitable dogfights. Sure enough, Messerschmitt fighters were escorting German bombers, and, in the ensuing fight, I was "hit." My tail was almost completely shot off, rendering my plane nearly impossible to control. I had to land my Yak immediately. Now, in a dogfight, there really isn't a set of predetermined rules. However, among most fighter pilots—regardless of whose side they are fighting for—once a guy is shot and his plane is going down, you leave him alone and go after another target. That's the only sensible thing to do.

For some reason unknown to me, the pilot who shot me did he not leave me alone; he followed right behind my sinking Yak like glue, while taking further shots at me. I turned around, and he was close enough to me that I could see him laughing. He was just toying with me, and he continued to target me right up until just before I reached the base. Needless to say, my plane was a wreck. I landed roughly on the field and— perhaps understandably—his actions made me very angry. I became so furious that I immediately hopped out of my plane, ran full speed at another waiting Yak and jumped eagerly in one motion into the cockpit. I was determined to get some payback.

I took off and headed back to the air combat zone with one goal in mind. Recognizing the German pilot's plane, I circled at full throttle, and when I came out of the turn, I was heading straight for him face to face. We were now engaged in a chicken fight. I did not want to make the kill until I knew he could recognize me. Even though he was firing at me and some bullets were hitting my plane, I did not return fire. For a few seconds, we could see each other. I knew then that I was no stranger to him. He sneered at me, as if to say that he was not going to turn away. I was still so mad at that point that, no matter what, I was not going to turn away either—even if it meant a direct front-to-front hit.

At the very last split second, he began to turn to my right. I had anticipated this and blasted the back half of his plane. He was no longer in control, so I pulled up hard while twisting so that, when I came out of the pull, I was behind him. I emptied every bullet in my machine gun chambers even after his plane blew up in the air. I circled and watched with satisfaction as the bits and pieces of both him and his plane fell to the ground. I felt no remorse; such is the brutality of war.

As I was flying face to face with the German pilot, I had a flashback to when as a youngster I had experienced the same feeling: the desire for revenge, the need for payback.

We had a professor when I was in the gymnasium, the equivalent of high school. It just so happened that this professor was German. His name was Hilarious Bristinger. At that time, the fact that he was German was not a big deal because it was before the war started. This teacher was not in the profession because he loved to teach or because he loved kids. He was in it strictly for the money. As a matter of fact, he was usually in a bad mood and was always rude to me and to my classmates. We got the impression that Professor Bristinger didn't like us.

During recess breaks and after eating lunch, we guys would kick around a few soccer balls. We would have two or three balls going and try to control one ball or take away the balls from one another. Quite often we would make up two teams by taking turns picking players and play each other. It was just for fun, but it was so much fun that most of us would arrive at school early so that we would have some soccer time before school started. Almost every morning, as Professor Bristinger arrived at school, he would zero in on one of the soccer balls, take a run at it and kick that ball off the field. Naturally, he aimed for the furthest places and the areas with tall grass and trees so that finding one of his kicked balls was always a chore. We would take turns retrieving the kicked ball and quite often that kid would end up being late for the first class.

This routine was beginning to be a real annoyance and was constantly taxing our patience. One day I came up with a scheme we hoped would stop Bristinger's ball-kicking nonsense or at least send a message to this professor.

A group of us, five in total including myself, pitched in some money and on a non-school day went to one of the smaller towns nearby. We found an ironsmith and custom-ordered a steel ball fabricated to the exact shape and size of a soccer ball. When the steel soccer ball was ready, I brought it home and painted it the same colour as one of our soccer balls. My artwork was successful. When I was finished with the steel ball, it looked exactly like a regular soccer ball. The steel ball now had acquired a perfectly matching light brown hue and even the painted stitching looked authentic.

My plan was to place the steel ball almost on the professor's path towards the bench on the side of the field. We also had a large rock similar in colour, and we placed it near the steel ball in case we needed an explanation. We thought we could switch the steel ball with the rock and our plot would not be discovered. We figured, if need be, that we could always claim that the professor had kicked the brown rock by mistake.

We made our way to the field and went about playing a soccer game: team versus team so that only one ball was in play. The professor made his way onto the field and, of course, just like clockwork, when he saw that brown steel soccer ball, he made a mad run and kicked it. Instantly, as his foot made contact with the steel soccer ball, he let out an ear-piercing scream and immediately fell to the ground, clutching it. In the meantime, we quickly swapped the steel soccer ball with the brown rock. We went to the principal to report that the professor had been running, stumbled on a rock, and was currently lying by the field nearly unconscious from pain.

After school we buried the steel ball in a secluded area in the woods and placed twigs and leaves over the ground as camouflage.

The professor was taken away to the hospital in a wagon, and we didn't see him for over two weeks. He returned to teach wearing a cast on his foot, but he wasn't the same. He knew that we had done something and that it wasn't a rock that he'd kicked but he couldn't figure it out nor did he have any proof. Bristinger finished the rest of the year, scowling and evidently miserable most of the time, and he didn't return the following year.

When the war ended, I was still flying. During this final period of the war, the Russian forces were no longer well-organized. It was kind of an "every man for himself" type of offensive that we were engaged in. Operating with the sense that it would soon be over, since the German resistance was decreasing exponentially, our goals were basically to kill as many German pilots and soldiers as possible and to inflict as much damage as we could on what was left of their military infrastructure.

Germany officially capitulated on May 8, 1945, thereafter referred to as V-Day. The ceremonial signing took place the day before in Reims, France, and in Berlin's eastern suburbs just after midnight, with General Nikolai Puchov and General Zhukov heading up the Allied delegation and Field Marshal Wilhelm Keitel signing for Germany. Keitel, grim-faced at the event, then resigned and later would be hanged for his crimes. Victory in Europe was sealed at last.

Although this ended Russia's war against Germany, it did nothing to stem Stalin's brutality against his own people. Now motivated by paranoia, Stalin arrested his top general Nikolai Puchov and tortured others until they would testify against him. General Mikhail Myryaga, the hero of Berlin, was arrested and sentenced to 25 years. Another forty top generals were arrested and imprisoned until Stalin's death. Any Russian prisoner of war who had been freed and returned was considered to be a deserter and was either shot or sent to the Gulag for many years (or even a lifetime) of hard labour. For Stalin it was simple; no Russian was allowed to surrender. To Stalin, a man who had become a prisoner had disobeyed him.

Marshal Georgy Zhukov was the most important and most successful Russian general in World War II. He was responsible for the successful defence of Moscow, Stalingrad, and Leningrad against German forces, eventually pushing them back to Germany. He led the final attack on Berlin and was so popular after the war that Stalin, feeling threatened, demoted him and moved him to obscure regional commands.

There was a lot of confused activity in the air, where military planes were still flying. Most of the visible bombers were from England. We would wave or salute as we passed one another, and as long as the plane wasn't a German one, everything was fine. Every now and then, we encountered a defiant surviving Messerschmitt; however, those sightings became more and more scarce, and those pilots did not last very long.

I found out about the end of the war one day after I landed, and my comrades told me that Germany had surrendered, and the war was over. At the time I didn't know what date it was; as a matter of fact, I didn't even know what month it was. When asked, I was told by one of them that it was May 7, in the west and May 9, in the east. My first thought was that I would be able to begin to search for my parents right away, but in actual fact this was delayed because of my new orders. I was bound for Moscow in order to participate in the victory celebrations and to receive my medal for being a "Hero of the Soviet Union"—my fourth Red Star.

Shortly thereafter, I was in Moscow, standing in line with a few of the other distinguished representatives of Russia's military finest. Stalin was present as well. When the time came for me to receive my medal, the master of ceremonies began reading aloud to the crowd a list of all my achievements—at least those that were on record. As he was reading this long list of my deeds, I remember wondering, "When did I manage to get the time to do all this?" It eludes me to this day. I received recognition for my outstanding work with the Special Forces and was credited with bringing in six German officers; many they had no use for and the ones I killed did not count. The emcee continued to recount my successful involvement with the partisans, even though I had received a 30-year suspended sentence in one of the missions; they didn't mention that at the ceremony.

The emcee also praised my "hunting business," as it was called. "hunting" mostly involved flying solo. Usually, I used a Polikarpov for those missions because I had to turn off the engine so the enemy would not hear me, and the Polikarpov was better suited to fly than a Yak for this purpose. A hunting mission was designed to destroy units resting on the ground—moving tanks and trucks, railway cars, or anything else in the enemy's arsenal.

Once I spotted a target, I would turn off the engine and begin to glide and swoop down upon the target, while experiencing flashbacks…and feeling the same exhilaration I felt in my cadet glider training. Often the enemy would see the plane and fire, but it would be too late. By the time they turned to shoot, it was over. Sometimes, I would drop grenades or often shoot them up. Once I tied five grenades together and dropped them directly onto the top of a tank. When I turned to check the results, I could see one of the tracks had blown off and the tank was burning. I took pride in my accomplishments, but I could never stay around too long to gloat.

By the end of the war, I had 24 confirmed and four unconfirmed kills of enemy fighter planes, either shot down or destroyed on the ground. I also blew up two strategic enemy fuel depots. Until then, I had never thought much about the actual number of kills, because I had been too occupied with the task of simply annihilating as many German bastards as I could. To this day, I still feel that I didn't kill enough of them.

CHAPTER 26

Endgame

By the end of World War II, over 75 million people had lost their lives and millions more were displaced. In Berlin during the endgame, the final days before Germany's unconditional surrender to Russia and the Allies, guerrilla-war battles were taking place between the invading Russians and German defenders that included civilians as young as 12 years of age. All the experienced German soldiers had previously been sent to the front. Any male who would not fight the Russians was immediately shot or hanged.

General Dwight D. Eisenhower, now in command of the most powerful allied forces representing 16 countries, did not want to risk any more casualties—plus he wanted to prevent the Russians from advancing into Denmark, so he left the battle for Berlin to the Russians. This resulted in over 300,000 Russian soldiers giving up their lives, and over 100,000 German casualties. As well, 480,000 German soldiers were taken prisoner. The ultimate goal was to conquer Berlin, find and capture Hitler, and take control of the Reich Chancellery, Hitler's official residence from where he had waged a good part of the war. Stalin insisted that the Russian flag would be raised atop the Reich Chancellery by the beginning of the May Day celebrations on May 1, 1945.

Located near the Reich Chancellery was the *Führerbunker*. The *Führerbunker* was part of a subterranean air-raid shelter and bunker complex. Hitler moved into that underground bunker in mid-January, 1945 and ran his regime from there, up until he and Eva Braun committed suicide there on April 30. Just the day before, Hitler had married Eva Braun, had written his last will and testament, and appointed Grand

Admiral Karl Dönitz his successor. Even in his final words Hitler blamed the Reich's failure on the Jews.

During the entire war, Hitler had actually spent very little time in Berlin, as it had become so dangerous for him. For the last years, he had no real headquarters to speak of. Basically, wherever Hitler stayed became his de facto headquarters. He spent a great deal of the wartime at the *Berghof*, his home in the Bavarian Alps, and at least 800 days during the war at the *Wolfsschanze* (the Wolf's Lair) which was a top-secret high security site in the Masurian Woods near a small East Prussian town called Rastenburg, now part of Poland. In spite of all the high security, it was at this Wolf's Lair where Klaus von Stauffenberg carried out what was the most formidable assassination attempt on Hitler's life.

During the last days of the war, Hitler was leading a fight that had already been lost. He did not believe his generals' reports that Germany's armies were either overcome or on the verge of defeat and that the allies were on their way to completely surrounding Berlin. His mind had reached a state of delusional and almost complete insanity. Regardless of Hitler's own delusions, General Eisenhower's combined allied forces were now approaching Berlin from the west, through Italy from the south and over 2.5 million Russian forces were approaching Berlin from the east.

On April 25, 1945, the American soldiers and their Russian counterparts met at the River Elbe, 60 kilometers southeast of Berlin. They shared a dinner dubbed "whisky meets vodka." Eisenhower decided that a race to Berlin between the Americans and the British would sour their relations. He was also reluctant to expose his troops to more casualties, both from defending Germans and friendly fire by Russians from the east. Eisenhower also had been receiving reports that the Germans were preparing to launch a final massive attack from Hitler's home in the Bavarian Alps. Eisenhower wanted to save his troops for that possibility. These and multiple factors caused his decision to let the Russians take Berlin. This decision angered Field Marshal Bernard Law Montgomery, who stood on the Rhine with visions of triumphantly entering Berlin, and did not trust the Russians as they had been setting up puppet regimes in the countries they had liberated. Montgomery headed north to Denmark and successfully cut off the Russian advance. He did not want to allow Stalin control of the Baltic region. The mistrust of Stalin by the allies was intensifying daily.

On April 27, 1945, the Italian fascist dictator Benito Mussolini was captured by Italian partisans. Mussolini was disguised as a German soldier as part of a convoy heading to the Swiss Alps. On route to Switzerland in a small town called Dongo near Lake Como, Urbano Lazaro, one of the partisans spotted Mussolini and arrested him. The partisans soon discovered that Mussolini's mistress, Claretta Petacci, was also part of the convoy, and she too was subsequently detained.

The next day, Mussolini and Petacci while being chauffeured to Milan in order to stand trial, the car in which they were being transported came to a stop at the village Giulino di Mezzegra. Another partisan, Walter Audisio who went by his "nom de guerre" Colonel Valerio, shot them both in cold blood. Their bodies were hung by their ankles at an Esso gas station in the Piazzale Loreto in Milan for all to see. Their corpses were beaten, shot at, and hit with hammers.

Allegations soon followed that Winston Churchill had been directly involved in the assassination of Mussolini. It would come out that Churchill had previously sent a letter to Mussolini outlining a plan for England and Italy to finalize a truce with the intent of joining forces in order to invade the Soviet Union. Apparently, Churchill could not afford to take the chance that Mussolini was still in possession of said letter and could use that letter against him…so Churchill ordered Mussolini's assassination and destruction of the letter, so the rumor went.

Meanwhile the residents of Berlin had very little food, no gas, no electricity and no running water. The people were hoping that the Americans or the British would come first. They had no knowledge of Eisenhower's strategy and inevitably suffered the consequences and wrath of the Russians entering their homeland. Because of the vicious atrocities perpetrated by the Germans on their people, the Russians invaded with revenge in their hearts. During the daytime they fought, house by house; during the night the invading Russian soldiers intoxicated themselves with alcohol, stole and looted, and raped and murdered thousands of innocent civilians. Numerous Berlin citizens committed suicide; mostly they were young girls who were afraid of being raped or ones who had become rape victims and could not endure the shame. Drunkenness became ubiquitous.

As previously mentioned, Hitler and Eva Braun committed suicide on April 30, 1945, in mid-afternoon. Eva bit on a cyanide capsule; Hitler shot himself in the head as he did the same. Their bodies were wrapped in blankets, taken outside to the garden, dosed with petrol, and set on fire. These were Hitler's final wishes as he did not want to suffer the same indignities as Mussolini.

Their charred remains were found by the Russians after the war and were secretly buried in Magdeburg, Germany, along with Joseph Goebbels and his family. In 1970, by order of supreme leader Leonid Brezhnev, the KGB exhumed their remains, burned and crushed them thoroughly and scattered the residue in the Ehle River near Biederitz. All that the Russians kept, or so the story goes, were Hitler's teeth and a piece of his skull where the bullet hole was.

In the evening on April 30th, 1945, Russian troop division 150 led by platoon commander Vasily Ustyugov made its way into the Reichstag. There ensued the vicious final battle…the Russians desperate to raise their flag atop the building, and the Germans fighting zealously for survival. That battle raged on as the Russians inched their way to control more real estate in the Reichstag. There were no lights, so when darkness arrived it became even more difficult to advance because there was a lot of friendly fire. This happened on both sides. One had to be extremely careful. In war, they say capturing the last territory is the hardest.

Shortly before 11 p.m. on April 30, 1945, the Russians finally prevailed. At 10:40 p.m., one of Ustyugov's men, Rakhimzhan Qoshqarbaev, climbed up the building and inserted the Russian flag in the crown of the female statue of "Germania" atop the Reichstag. A Soviet war photographer, Viktor Temin, persuaded Marshal Zhukov to allow him to take of picture of the event from the air. After taking the picture from the plane, Viktor Temin continued on to Moscow without permission so that he could have this famous picture published before anyone else. The next day Temin returned to Berlin with several copies of *Pravda* with his picture on the front page.

Raising the Russian flag over the Reichstag

To this day there is controversy over details of the first flag-raising event. Some historians believe that it was too dark to take a good quality photo of the initial flag raising and that the initial picture did not include any soldiers; it merely depicted the Russian flag atop the Reichstag, so it was re-enacted on May 2, and another picture taken by a Jewish Russian war photographer Yevgeny Khaldei, became the famous photo described as one of the most symbolic photographs taken throughout the entire war.

On May 2, 1945, Berlin finally surrendered to the Russians. Approximately 1 million German soldiers put down their arms. Two days later on May 4, Field Marshal Montgomery accepted the unconditional surrender of German forces in northwest Germany and Denmark, including all naval vessels operating in those regions.

Next, on a special mission assigned to Allied Forces' Easy Company by Eisenhower, the troops reached Hitler's home in the Bavarian Alps anticipating a final bloody battle with SS troops. To their surprise and relief, German forces had abandoned the town of Berchtesgaden and the allied troops captured the territory without firing a single shot. En route,

Easy Company passed thousands of German soldiers fleeing to the west. None wanted to be captured by the Russians and were hoping to surrender to the Americans or the British.

On May 7, 1945, at Allied headquarters in Reims, France, following the orders of Dönitz, Colonel General Alfred Jodl signed the unconditional surrender of all German forces. President Franklin D. Roosevelt was present to sign for the Allies. The order came into effect at 11 p.m. on May 8, 1945, thus officially ending the war in Europe. The ceremonial German capitulation is signed just after midnight on May 9, 1945.

CHAPTER 27

The "Horned Ones"

To this day the Russians will not admit it. If not for the "Horned Ones"—the Americans—I am 100 per cent certain that Russia would never have won the war against Germany.

In early 1942, I was assigned to fly to Alaska with another pilot and pick up two American *P-King Cobra* fighter planes and deliver them back to a Russian base. The other pilot, Vladimir (surname unknown) and I took off from a base in Northeast Russia, flying in a decrepit *Polikarpov P-o2*. This model had two open individual cabs, so we could shout at each other for communication purposes. When we arrived at the American Air Force base, we were greeted by a friendly group of maintenance workers. One of these American crew members spoke Russian. Vladimir and I were immediately escorted to the two awaiting planes, their engines already running. En route to the planes, Vladimir came close by my side and whispered in my ear with disbelief, "They don't have any horns!" At that moment, in a confounding revelation, I realized that Vladimir did in fact believe that Americans had horns, and if he believed it, then it would also make sense that many other Russians believed that as well.

The Americans had been reluctant to become involved in the war in Europe. That changed on December 7, 1941, when Japan—while executing a ruse in pretending to show intention of peaceful negotiations—attacked US naval bases at Pearl Harbor. As a matter of fact, two Japanese representatives (Ambassador Kochisaburō Nomura and Saburō Kurusu) were meeting with US Secretary of State Cordell Hull while the attacks occurred. The following day, President Roosevelt gave his famous "a date which will live in infamy" speech and declared war against the Imperial Empire of Japan. Roosevelt worded that speech in a precise manner in order to evoke the most dramatic and profound effect. He was extremely successful in achieving that goal. The "Day of Infamy" speech was heard by an unprecedented 81 per cent of the population. In just a little over half an hour after Roosevelt's speech, the US Congress formally passed a declaration of war against Japan. American men and women were signing up to fight the Japanese like never before.

Previously, Hitler had made an oral agreement with Japan that Germany would declare war against United States; however, Hitler was not certain how that war would be engaged. The attack on Pearl Harbor actually surprised Hitler. Nevertheless, the event did answer the question. Japanese Ambassador Hiroshi Ōshima met with German Foreign Minister Joachim von Ribbentrop on December 8, 1941, to seek a firm commitment from Germany that a formal declaration of war against the United States would ensue. Germany's foreign minister, was aware that Germany had no obligation to fulfill this demand under the terms of the Tripartite Pact, in which Germany promised help only if Japan was attacked and not if Japan was the aggressor. Von Ribbentrop did not want another enemy. Hitler's thoughts were different. Hitler believed that Japan was much mightier than it actually was and was confident that once America was defeated, Japan would help Germany with the war against Russia. Consequently, Hitler declared war on United States three days later, on December 11, 1941. His belief in Japanese superiority never materialized.

The Americans were already sending planes and other weaponry to England, but now they were committed in a much bigger way. An abundant and continuous flow of supplies kept arriving in Russia from America via the Arctic. The Americans supplied Russia with planes, tanks, trucks, ammunition, food, and staples such as coffee, chocolate and cigarettes. As long as it was to aid "Uncle Joe," the Americans kept sending arms and provisions. None of their aid was as important as the communication devices. The Americans paid dearly to deliver those supplies, as many a ship was destroyed by German air attacks and U-boat submarines. Thousands of American soldiers were killed attempting to traverse the Arctic route.

Before receiving the American radios, the Russian army used human runners in the battlefield to send and receive information as far as three to four kilometers away. Before receiving the upgraded, American-made radios, those used by the Russians at the front were not very reliable, and they weighed approximately 40 to 50 kilos. It was like having a guy on your back. Most of those radios were also not wireless, so if you wanted to talk with someone you needed to have wires connecting them. If it was a wireless radio, the Germans had the technical ability to send out jamming signals rendering the Russian radios ineffective. Upon listening to a message sent by an ally, one would pick up all sorts of background noise and interference. It was very difficult to accurately decipher an exact message, so again the runners would be put into action. These runners would be carrying notes to and from commanders at the front and that was the main means of keeping in contact with one another.

Once the Russians acquired the American-made radios, their power could also be easily intensified by a man pedaling on a bicycle-type generator. These radios were very dependable, and the Germans could not jam their signals. Communication improved immensely, and reconnaissance was becoming more and more effective.

After the war, when I was living in Canada, there was a television show in the '60s called "Gilligan's Island." On that show, the main character, Gilligan, seemed always to be pedaling a bicycle in order to help generate power to the array of batteries that the professor character assembled. Where the bicycle came from and why there were always so many batteries on that deserted island is one question that came to mind; however, every time I saw the Gilligan character pedaling, I smiled to myself as I experienced a flashback to those Russian soldiers frantically pedaling away in order to boost the signal strength of those battle service radios supplied by the Americans. In my special combat missions, usually masquerading as a partisan, I delivered many of those radios to the frontlines.

As well as supplying the United Kingdom and Russia with weapons and materials, the Americans were the instigators of the D-Day invasion at Normandy. Without that invasion, Germany could have concentrated more manpower and weaponry against the Russians. In a sense, Germany was now facing opposition on three fronts. American aid and direct involvement were part of each of those fronts; Americans supplied bombers to England, which attacked Germany from the northwest, and Americans supplied radios, planes, staples and weaponry to Russia attacking from the east. The United States also had hundreds of thousands of troops on the ground fighting against Italian forces from the south, allied with England and Canada as well as other allied forces from the west. It was the Americans who also took out the V1 and V2 rocket production facilities and launching sites. The entire outcome of the war would have been altered if Germany had had free reign to fire those *Vergeltungswaffen* (retaliatory weapons) rockets into Russia.

Hitler was in many ways a brilliant strategist; however, he did make many mistakes. Sometimes small decisions can change an entire outcome. Earlier, Germany was in fact winning the air war with Britain and was just about to deliver the final and decisive blows when two German pilots mistakenly bombed London. Churchill immediately retaliated by bombing Berlin. Hitler was so angry that he discontinued all other air attacks on England and focused entirely on destroying London. This gave the RAF time to rebuild damaged airfields, train new pilots and repair aircraft. These new opportunities helped Britain to win the "Battle of Britain" and to prevent land invasions by Germany on her soil.

At the onset of the conflict, in 1941, Stalin was controlling all the military strategy, often with devastating consequences. Towards the end, Stalin began listening to his generals and allowed them to hold their ground or retreat and regroup (only on Stalin's authority) instead of constantly attacking. Hitler did the opposite and maintained his policy never to retreat. That policy directly caused the slaughter of hundreds of thousands of his troops.

Towards the end of the war, Hitler was sending armies that did not even exist on the offensive. He was becoming increasingly unbalanced at this point, which led to the plot by Claus von Stauffenberg, orchestrated in July 1944, to kill Hitler and take over Berlin.

Stalin, meanwhile, was a vain and ruthless megalomaniac. Most believed that Stalin loved no one except maybe his first wife Ekaterina Svanidze who died of typhus at the age of 22. Stalin's second wife, Nadezhda Alliluyeva, was found dead with a revolver by her side in 1932 after a fight with Stalin. For the sake of Stalin's reputation, it would be reported that she died of appendicitis. Sixty years later it was found to be suicide, and yet suspicion still remained that Stalin had killed her.

Stalin's son Yakov Dzhugashvili served as an artillery officer in the Red Army and was captured on July 16, 1941, during the early stages of the German invasion of Russia at the Battle of Smolensk. In August Stalin sentenced Yakov's wife, his own daughter-in-law, to two years hard labor in the Gulag according to *General Order 270*.

The Germans later offered to exchange Yakov for German Field Marshal Friedrich Paulus captured by the Soviets at the Battle of Stalingrad, but Stalin turned the offer down, allegedly saying, "I will not trade a marshal for a lieutenant." Soon after that, Yakov killed himself.

In some ways, I think the Russian population was experiencing a kind of universal victim's syndrome, in the sense that just after Germany invaded Russia, Stalin managed to regain their support and galvanized them into eager willingness to fight for him.

Before the invasion the Russian people had just gone through WW1, then a revolution, and a bloody civil war. Then they had to endure the death of Lenin in 1924. Lenin was aware that he was going to die and was assessing his potential successors. Leon Trotsky and Joseph Stalin were at the top of the list. Before his death Lenin wrote a letter condemning Stalin's character and suggested that his position of general secretary be taken from him. The letter was kept secret and Stalin prevailed. Stalin then had Trotsky deported from Russia. Soon after, on Stalin's orders, an assassin named Ramón Mercader assassinated Trotsky in Mexico.

In the beginning, the people all worshiped Stalin. When the massacres and purges ensued, the people began to fear him. Stalin was paranoid to the point of mental illness. He had three apartments at the Kremlin. He arranged daily to have three sets of breakfasts, lunches and dinners; those meals would be left at the door of each of those apartments. By doing so, Stalin believed it would be harder for anyone to know what door he would come out of in order to eat, thus making any attempt on his life harder. He also ordered that the curtains at any place he stayed in be cut one meter above the floor and that all the snow outside his windows be kept fresh so he could see if there were any tracks.

Once the collectives began in the late 1920's, over 3 million people were imprisoned or exiled. Over 10 million peasants were forced off their land and over 7 million were killed by enforced famine—5 million of those were from the Ukraine. Another million people were executed during the "Great Terror." Millions of others were sent to work as slaves in the gulags.

Most of them died as well. When all was said and done, Stalin had killed over 20 million of his own people before the war started. Stalin also purged his own army by executing over 40,000 officers, but meanwhile kept training Germans to drive tanks and to fly airplanes. In that way, he was acting as a traitor to himself. In 1939 once Poland was defeated, Stalin killed over 22,000 of their officers.

When Germany occupied Ukraine during the first few months of the war, people thought of the Germans as saviors, and so collaboration with the Nazis was the norm. Over a million Ukrainians served with Germany. The Germans also dug up thousands of graves, revealing the slaughter of Russians by the NKVD. Many Ukrainians joined the SS and were sent off to the war front to round up Red Army Russian stragglers.

Germany encouraged the settling of scores and the informing on any communists or followers of Stalin. The Germans also fueled anti-Semitism by promoting the "Master Race," which also allowed the massacre of disabled people.

In spite of all the mistakes Hitler made—underestimating the Russian winters, forming allegiances with really bad military allies like Italy, Hungary, Romania, and even Japan—if not for America entering the war, Germany would have been able to concentrate the bulk of its forces on Russia and would have defeated her. Japan really did Russia a favor by attacking America and "awakening the sleeping giant."

The Americans teamed up with the Brits and the Canadians causing Italy to surrender on September 8, 1943. As a result, Hitler had to redeploy forces from both the Western and Eastern Fronts thus weakening his entire Army.

The importance of the Americans getting into the war could not be understated. American General George S. Patton led the US 7th Army in its invasion of Sicily and swept across northern France at the head of its 3rd Army in the summer of 1944. Later that same year, Patton's forces played a key role in defeating the German counterattack in the Battle of the Bulge, after which he led them across the Rhine River and into Germany, capturing over 16,000 kilometres of territory and liberating the country from the Nazi regime.

American General Dwight D. Eisenhower was appointed supreme commander of the Allied Expeditionary Force in December of that year and given the responsibility of spearheading the planned Allied invasion of Nazi-occupied Europe. As previously mentioned, on June 6, 1944 (D-Day), more than 150,000 Allied forces crossed the English Channel and stormed the beaches of Normandy. This invasion led to the liberation of Paris on August 25 and turned the tide of the war in Europe decisively in favour of the Allies.

Another of the horned ones contributions to the cause was the *Mustang P-51* airplane. It is widely regarded as the finest all-around piston-engine fighter of World War II and was produced in significant numbers. Manufacturing the American built *Mustang P-51* fitted with the powerful Rolls-Royce Merlin engine gave the fighter outstanding high-altitude performance. With drop fuel tanks, the *Mustang P-51* had an operational range of more than 2,500 kilometres and mounted their first long-range bomber escort missions over Germany in mid-December 1943. They quickly outclassed Germany's premier fighters, destroying nearly 5,000 enemy aircraft.

The Merlin was already being produced under license in the United States by the Packard Motor Company, and by the summer of 1943, Packard Merlin-powered *Mustang P-51s* were coming off North American's assembly line. Merlin-powered *Mustang P-51s*, equipped with the ability to jettison fuel tanks worked extremely well against Germany's *Blitzkrieg*.

On March 6, 1944, over 800 US bombers, escorted by over 900 fighters, attacked Berlin. Known as "Black Monday," bomber losses were heavy, but this mission, and others like it, helped the Allies' goal of pulling the German fighters into the sky where the *Mustang P-51* could destroy them and establish air supremacy. Much to the dismay of the commander in-chief of the Luftwaffe, Hermann Göring, this helped to establish air supremacy by all the allies over the Germans near the end of the war, making life so much easier for Russian pilots directly impacting positively in all aspects of Russia's war with Germany.

The Mustang P-51 *Allied fighter plane*

Joseph Stalin, Franklin D. Roosevelt, and Winston Churchill at the Potsdam Conference

CHAPTER 28

Afterwards

As mentioned, I returned from Moscow to receive my fourth Red Star as "Hero of the Soviet Union" in a ceremony filled with pomp and circumstance; that medal was awarded to me by Stalin himself. Afterwards, my commanding officer called me in for an interview. He said I was to be released from duty the next day. I had the choice, he said, of being demobilized to become a regular Russian citizen or remaining in the air force. He did not mention, however, all of my suspended sentences. I figured that, if I chose to be demobilized, I would probably end up in a camp in a gulag somewhere in Siberia serving out all the suspended sentences. At this point, I had actually lost count, but the sentences imposed totaled sixty years, or more—enough that I would never enjoy another day of freedom for the rest of my life. As well, with no family to return to, I didn't really want to be a regular civilian either. I "volunteered" to stay in the air force.

At first, I mostly sat around in a bunkhouse that had previously been utilized as some sort of school. Eventually, I was assigned to pilot an important general—and, to this day, I cannot remember his name—around the region as he performed post-war diplomatic missions. As I still maintained my rank as a Special Forces captain and a commander, I was considered trustworthy and skilled enough to fly this general around.

When I reported to the airport to check out the plane I would be flying, I found that it was an overhauled four-engine *Tupolev TB-3* night-bomber. The interior had been converted into a passenger plane with seats and even had a sleeping place equipped with a Pullman. They provided me quarters at the airport where I resided and where I would be constantly on call. Whenever the general needed me, I would be summoned and expected to show up immediately ready to go. If I wanted to go somewhere (into town or to a movie, for example), I simply told the person in charge where I would be so that they could send someone to pick me up if I was summoned.

My first flight was to Hungary, landing in Budapest. Then we were off to Romania for another conference, where I stayed in a hotel for about four days. This way of life continued for about four or five months, and I found it all quite boring and uneventful. I suppose it was better than risking my life every day; however, many of the regions that the general visited were full of turmoil. Often, these were territories that had been occupied by the Germans or the Russians, and they were not yet formally an independent country. Furthermore, many of the citizens wanted revenge on all the collaborators, creating quite a messy situation. Citizens often broke the hands and feet of the collaborators, crippling them completely. I witnessed many women whose heads were being shaved and a lot of men being beaten severely. As collaborators had been plentiful, it ended up in many scenes of torture, humiliation, and often slaughter.

On a trip to France, I found the people very unfriendly. When the Germans had first marched into France, the Vichy Government partnered with them without delay and began rounding up Jews, the Roma people (often called gypsies), invalids, and mentally ill people—and then shipping them to German controlled camps. With no love lost between the French and the Russians, there were many accounts to settle. Payback can be horrible.

Over the next few months, many countries would be redefined as many were not yet sovereign nations. One day I flew to Warsaw, and suddenly it hit me. I was just sitting in that plane waiting. The general had been picked up in a car and was attending a conference of some sort, and I had a full tank of fuel. It was about mid-afternoon and getting hot. I was sitting, waiting; actually, I was reading something when it just struck me. "What the fuck am I doing here?" It was as if someone had come and turned on a light, or pushed me, or awakened me or something like that. And then I didn't even think further; I just acted on impulse.

I radioed the tower and received clearance for take-off and tower information about coordinates and an updated weather report. The guys in the tower had no idea where the general was. Had they known that I was alone, it would have been different. I knew I had enough fuel to make it to Berlin—to the Americans, so I taxied to the runway and took off. I also knew that they had me on the radar, so initially I took off in the correct direction, heading towards Moscow. After a while, I flew really low, almost scraping treetops in order to avoid radar detection, and then made a huge semi-circle until I was heading directly towards Berlin. I began wondering how the general would react when he found out that I was gone. The thought of a death sentence for desertion also occupied a good deal of my thoughts during that flight. Getting caught simply wasn't an option, but I felt I'd served the Russians long enough. It was definitely time for a change.

As I raised altitude on my approach to Zehlendorf Airport in Berlin, two American fighter pilots intercepted me. I was most certainly over the American zone, I thought. With one American fighter on each side of me, I could see the pilots looking me over. I assumed that they figured that I was a Russian pilot who had lost his way. After all, I was flying a Russian plane and still in my Russian uniform. Then they pointed me in the direction of the Russian zone of Berlin as if to show me where it was. I kept shaking my head no. Finally, they understood and both gave me a firm thumbs-down hand signal. When I think about it now, I realize Russians could have spotted me just as easily. Thankfully, few Russian planes were flying around Berlin at the time.

Joseph Halpern escaped from Russians in a Tupolev TB-3 *bomber*

The Russian zone bordered the American zone, and at that time the Russians and the Americans were friendly allies and even trusted one another. Russian soldiers would often travel into the American zone to visit the nightclubs and such. This was long before the building of the Berlin wall and the beginning of the Cold War, after some time, the only way to take supplies into Berlin's non-Russian sectors was by airplane, and this was happening on a regular basis, part of the *Marshall Plan* initiated by the American Secretary of State George Marshall in 1947. The Soviets didn't want to be a part of it so the Russian version, the *Molotov Plan* was initiated that same year. I landed at Zehlendorf Airport, and the American military police picked me up immediately in a jeep. They were already waiting for me with a guy who spoke both Russian and English. He asked, "What's going on? Did you make a mistake?"

"No. I want to stay here," I replied. Then they took me into detention, where I was interrogated for two days. They wanted to know everything: where I came from, what I had been doing during the war, where I was born, everything I could remember; you name it, they wanted to know. And so, I obliged them; I had no secrets and remembered a lot, so I told them everything they wanted to know. Many people were trying to get out of Russia at that point after the war. As a matter of fact, even one of my commanding officers had gotten out. I met him at a nightclub in New York years later and that's how I found out. He had recognized me from behind, and I heard "Hey, Joseph." When I turned around, I nearly saluted him even though we were both now civilians.

After passing the American inspection, I was brought before an officer of the Polish Air Force operating out of England. He asked me if I wanted to join the Polish Air Force, and I said that I did not.

"Because you are Jewish," he continued "we will place you in a Jewish displaced persons' (DP) camp." An American entered the room and told me that I would be treated just like an American GI and would have all the same privileges, and he gave me a "Can-carte." Once I arrived in the camp, this card enabled me to move in and out of the camp, get transportation outside on the buses or subway and receive meals. Possessing a Can-carte also enabled me to obtain other supplies at the supply depot. Compared to the rationing of goods outside the camp, the DP camp had an abundant supply of staples; I wanted for nothing.

Approximately 600 of us lived in the DP camp—families, men, women, and children, mostly Jews, from all over Europe awaiting settlement somewhere else. Cut off from the rest of the world, this "mini-city" had only one gate in and out, guarded by two American soldiers. The camp was surrounded by brick walls. Previously a military base, the camp consisted of a large central plaza with rooms and quarters sectioned off for families and singles alike. It had social clubs, orchestras, and theatres; performances occurred regularly. With so much to do, it was like one gigantic communal alliance. Food was abundant, with four kitchens in which people could get something to eat at any time of day or night, in addition to regular mealtimes. Officially, I resided in that DP camp throughout my stay in Berlin. Eventually, however, I lived in a villa just outside the city.

American soldiers came to the camp regularly for conversation and social activities. News reporters and various other information-seekers regularly questioned the survivors and took their pictures in order to document their experiences, especially those who had survived the death camps. After I became friends with quite a few other men, someone suggested that I might want to go outside the gates and get myself a nice place to live because many villas had been left empty after important Nazis or rich and famous people had left the city.

The thought of living in a nicer home, or even a mansion, appealed to me, so I made my way to the administration's real estate office and inquired. The fellow there gave me a list and simply said to choose any property on it. "Just move in and live there," he said. The villa I chose had a caretaker couple named Willie and Hilda. It was a huge place with about fourteen bedrooms. Of course, I made regular trips back to the camp for food and supplies.

While there were no restaurants to speak of, a few black market bistros sprang up eventually. The food they served was very good; one could order almost anything, provided it was ordered at least a day in advance. Even the mayor of Berlin ate regularly at one of those eateries.

The square at the DP camp served as a meeting place where residents gathered and shared the day's news. The movers and shakers met there, too, providing many opportunities and connections for enterprising businesspeople, smugglers, and black marketers. At first, I just hung around and listened to the propositions being made and deals going on.

One time, I overheard a guy saying that he had four submarines. As I eavesdropped, I heard another agree to purchase them and arrange for shipping. It was mind-boggling to see all the types of merchandise that exchanged hands in that square. Tanks, airplanes, ships, rocket launchers, grenades, all types of guns and ammunition—even a train engine with a set of railway cars; it was all for sale. At first, I believed some of these guys were a little bit cuckoo from shellshock or some other mental affliction sustained in combat. It was even more astonishing to realize that these deals were for real. It was as if these Jews were somehow controlling all the equipment and surplus left over from the war. The Americans didn't ship anything back home. Who knew where it all ended up? I know that Israel obtained some of that surplus because most of the trade was controlled by Jews. I assume not much got into unscrupulous hands.

Eventually, I got to know people better, and one man brought me into the black market butter trade. Other smugglers were melting vast quantities of butter in Poland and storing it in steel drums. We would drive to Poland, pick up those drums, and smuggle them back over the border to Berlin where we connected with the buyers and made the exchange. We were dealing in millions of marks. Each sector printed its own currency: there were American marks, English marks, French marks, and Russian marks—all of which were used to pay workers and to buy goods and services within the capital.

Ultimately, the goal was to convert marks into American dollars (at a ratio of about 2,000 marks to one dollar). Outside Germany, all the other European denominations were worth almost nothing. For example, we received about 12 million marks for each shipment of a dozen drums of butter. As it was impractical to sit and count millions of bills, we simply used the "squeeze method." Payments were made in burlap duffle bags filled with marks. A bag that was a bit loose was worth 3 million marks; one stuffed tight was the equivalent of 5 million marks; somewhere in the middle was worth 4 million marks. That's how we established our compensation.

Because I could speak Polish, I made connections with the guards at the border, and we eventually developed a hand sign so that we could drive right through. Of course, each border patrol received a cut of the action, too. I didn't need the money for my survival because I had a "Can-carte." At first, I was involved in such activities just to stay busy, and it was rather fun. Later on, I used my butter money to open up the orphanage and the proceeds from black market dealing would continue to go towards the kids who were fortunate enough to end up in the orphanage.

Because I could get various supplies with my "Can-carte," I also made money by selling this merchandise. I could get a pack of cigarettes and immediately sell it on the square for about 10,000 marks. I also gave the kids food, and I had a lot of fun in the nightclubs. After all, one carton of chocolate was worth about five nights on the town. Inside Germany, I could have been considered a rich man.

There were a few of us making money like that. One sold cigarettes, another chocolates, another condoms and nylons. The man with the nylons was rich—and also extremely popular with the women.

Joseph Halpern in post-war Berlin

CHAPTER 29

What Happened to Isabelle?

My life in the camp in Berlin was a rather pleasant one, but I was still bothered by the fate of my family and my girlfriend Isabelle—about whom I had heard nothing since the beginning of the war. I had made attempts during the war to find out where they were.

It was in the winter of 1941 that I felt an overpowering desire to find out what was going on at home. I took it upon myself to venture on a private mission to find Isabelle and my parents. After a combat air battle, I pretended that my plane was hit; I headed for my home and crashed my plane to justify my motives and reasons for not reporting for duty immediately after the dogfight. I joined forces with the partisans, who had seen me crash and hastily devised a plan to set free people in the detention camp near Vladimir Volynsky. I had been hearing about this camp for many months and felt I had to do something to help the people there.

The camp was in the woods just on the outskirts of town, and it had become a gathering place for people who were to be slaughtered. Later, people were tortured and beaten there. They would be forced to dig their own graves, ordered to disrobe, and then mowed down by machine gun fire as they stood by their freshly dug graves. After the war, mass graves sites were dug up all over the that area.

The night of my arrival under cover of darkness, the partisans and I blew up the four guard towers, killed all the guards inside and outside the encampment, and tore down the barbed-wire fence. Unfortunately, no one escaped from the camp that night. No one wanted to leave! The people in the camp were sickly, scared, and in denial.

I did not find Isabelle or my parents, nor could I find out any information about them. The detention camp near Vladimir Volynsky was quickly rebuilt. My mission had not been a success from any point of view. When the partisans returned me to my squadron, I told the commanders that I had been hit, lost control of the plane, veered off course, and crashed. For this, I received my first 30-year sentence for being absent from duty and was promptly returned to service. Ironically, later on I would receive a medal for bravery and for taking initiative on my impromptu mission. I did not have any other opportunities during the war to return to Vladimir Volynsky.

It was only after I had been in the displaced person's camp in Berlin for a while that I did find out what happened to Isabelle and most of the other Jewish girls in Vladimir Volynsky, as well as some of my male classmates.

One day in the camp, I ran into Aaron Kramer with whom I had gone to school. He had not been one of our group of cadets who had gone immediately into the air force at the beginning of the war, but I knew him fairly well. He had with him in the camp all kinds of pictures—which I copied and have kept to this day. Somehow, Aaron had managed to get out of Vladimir Volynsky alive. He joined up with the partisans and fought with them against the Germans until the end of the war.

The only other survivor I met from Vladimir Volynsky was named Gershon Katz, the younger brother of my good friend Joseph Katz. Gershon Katz had jumped out of a moving truck that was transporting victims to the camp in order to be shot or subjected to a worse fate. He had fled into the woods, dodging rifle fire as he ran. The Germans stopped the truck and thoroughly searched the woods for him. No escape attempt would be tolerated, and the Germans were always eager to show examples of what would happen to those who attempted it. However, Gershon escaped and later joined up with the partisans—and like Aaron Kramer—ended up in that DP camp with me in Berlin.

The three of us hung out quite a lot together in that camp. Of the approximately 11,000 or so Jewish people from Vladimir Volynsky, about eighty families had been sent to the Siberian gulag for not complying with passport acquisition in 1939. Of those eighty families, I heard that some had survived. Out of those 11,000 Jews from my hometown—except for those who survived the Gulag—the only known survivors were Aaron Kanter, Gershon Katz, and me. I soon found out from these two what became of Isabelle. I had to wait much longer before I discovered anything about my parents.

In 1941 the Russians separated the good-looking girls from the others and said they were going to be "put to work." They ended up as sex slaves to the Ukrainians, who were now collaborating with the Germans. The few commanding officers were the only Germans left in that region, and the Ukrainian collaborators were running the process. They were well armed; they were the ones who rounded up the Jews, transported the Jews, and tortured and beat up the Jews. Women and children were collected first; a child who cried on route was shot immediately. Steel bars that had been used to break up ice were now being used to bash in the heads of people in the camp in those woods. People were drowning in their own blood. The Ukrainians themselves committed the executions and mass murders.

In Berlin, I ran into a Ukrainian who had managed to get out before the Germans had left. This man, his wife, and another male friend of his somehow smuggled themselves into Romania and hid out with Gypsies for the duration of the war. He desperately wanted to escape because he had witnessed many of the atrocities committed by his countrymen and could not endure it any more psychologically. He had a lot of Jewish friends and felt compelled to help get them out of there. I had remembered seeing him around, as a customer at my grandfather's lumber business. Though I do not remember his name, I had recollections of him with my grandfather, so I believed that he was telling me the truth.

This Ukrainian told me that he saw another Ukrainian named Hitsko take my Isabelle, keep her in his house for about a week, then throw her dead body out of the house—unceremoniously leaving her broken body lying there in the street. One could only imagine what horrible things happened to her in that last week of life. After hearing this story, I was overcome with grief and rage.

This man told me that Hitsko was in Germany somewhere. With a lot of cooperation from the Americans and much persistence, I found Hitsko's address.

At that time, there was a group called "the Avengers" in Berlin. This group "took care of" anyone known to have been involved with the killing of Jews. It was a group of about thirty Jewish guys formed just after the war. Before the War of Independence broke out in Israel, all the members of "the Avengers" went to Israel to join the *Haganah*, which later became the *Massad*.

Meanwhile, I tracked down Hitsko and observed his residence and his activities for several days. Once I was certain that he was the man I had been looking for, I met with a representative of the Avengers, who was always gathering information, leads, and tips at the DP camp. I told this Avenger what Hitsko had done. We went back to Hitsko's residence together and met up with him. Once we were alone, the Avenger asked him, "Do you know why you are about to be killed?"

Before waiting for an answer, the Avenger continued, "You are to be killed because you are guilty of the rape, torture, and killing of Isabelle Perell." I relished the look of fear on his face, while I slowly killed Hitsko with my bare hands.

Joseph's first passionate love was Isabelle Perell

CHAPTER 30

A Promise Is a Promise

One morning while I was sitting in the main congregation area of the DP camp a sense of incompletion suddenly overwhelmed me; it was a profound eureka moment. The best way I can describe the occurrence was as if I had just been struck by lightning. I hadn't thought about the promise that I had made to Sergei Kargopolski, Sophie's father, for a long time. As I stood up, I spoke out loud to myself, "A promise is a promise."

I immediately walked to my quarters and began packing. Included in my luggage were my Russian captain's uniform, my Soviet documents, and some money…American, German and Russian currency. Just like that, I was on my way to Alma-Ata, in Kazakhstan to fulfill my promise to Sergei. After all, he had saved my life.

An American pilot flew me to Warsaw where I changed into my Russian uniform and began my four-day train journey back to Alma-Ata. I needed to find Sophie and get her out of Russia. I knew that I would once again be risking my life because being caught by the Russians would have meant certain execution. If the authorities connected me with any of my outstanding charges, it would mean immediate implementation of my death sentence.

I boarded the train in Warsaw. The main check points were in Minsk and Moscow. Those were the places where I had to rely heavily on my Special Forces training. I had to be as non-conspicuous as possible. Utilizing these special training techniques, I had become a master at the ability to blend in with a crowd and become almost invisible. This task was, however, increasingly difficult, clothed as I was in my Russian uniform. As well, mastering the "blending in" technique was more of a challenge for me because of my flaming red hair. Wearing my army cap was quite often the easiest solution. Nevertheless, the Special Forces commando training once again proved invaluable on this very personal and important mission.

In order to arrive alive and hook up with Sophie, I approached the situation and my ultimate objective just as if I were on a covert special operation. Many situations came up upon during which I had to depend on my training, my wits, some good fortune and occasionally…good old-fashioned bribery. Even in southeast Russia, American dollars were highly sought after.

In the end, I did manage to find Sophie. She was still working as a nurse in the veterans' hospital and she was vehemently determined to find a way to leave Russia. When asked about her feelings on the matter she replied fervently, "Let's get the hell out of here!"

I waited until the end of Sophie's shift then we went together to her apartment where we spent the night. I slept on the couch. In the morning, I awoke to the aroma of fresh coffee. She made us some breakfast, she packed a suitcase, and we began our journey together back to Berlin.

Sometimes during the trip back to the DP camp situations arose requiring that Sophie and I pretend to be a married couple. In other circumstances, we acted the role of brother and sister. Many situations required quick thinking on the fly and the utilization of cunning instincts. I was immensely relieved and pleasantly surprised to witness how proficient Sophie was at adapting to situations. Generally, the trip back went surprisingly well. Having said that, in retrospect, if not for my captain's rank, I do not believe we would have made the passage successfully.

Upon arriving back at the DP camp, our American curator suggested that we would be better off as husband and wife…at least on paper. He understood our situation very well, so even though we were officially on the books as a married couple, he did manage to find separate quarters for Sophie, and I continued my roles in the smuggling operation and spent a lot of time in the nightspots in Berlin. At the same time, Sophie and I became good friends.

CHAPTER 31

Lots of Kids Running Around

There were a lot of kids were running around the DP camp, often unsupervised. Mostly they were orphans of Jewish descent. There were kids of all sizes and of all ages, even some babies. So, I thought, "Why not use one of those left-over, abandoned German villas and organize a special place for those kids?" I began talking to a few women, and most showed genuine interest. One in particular, Clara Winters, a nurse by profession, and her husband, Rubin, became quite enthusiastic about the idea. Eventually, she became the head nurse and he became one of the main patrons of the project. I had been friends with an American-born German fellow serving as the reverend for the Americans. His name was Reverend Rotendorf and he became so fired up about the idea that, immediately we began looking together for a suitable place for the kids. In a matter of days, we had found one called *Schlachtensee*, a villa just on the outskirts of Berlin that the Gestapo had used during the war.

My American pal, Jim Black, heard about what we were doing, and he too wanted to help these kids. Later, he became instrumental in managing aid from the United States Army and the soldiers stationed in Berlin. It was amazing how fast the pieces fell into place.

The villa was a brick building equipped with a public address sound system, a large central area, and an auditorium with a stage. Later on, we actually installed a movie theatre in the auditorium. Eventually, we started moving in supplies, we created a dorm in the central area and we found Dr. Fishbain who would provide medical care. The Americans provided kitchen utensils and supplied food and other necessary commodities.

One day we moved the beds from the DP camp, loaded the kids up in buses and brought them to their new home. I named the institution the Herzl Orphanage, in honour of Theodor Herzl, the founder of the Zionist movement, and was now open for business. Permanent staff moved in, and Rotendorf visited regularly, bringing many provisions from the US army and other benefactors.

At full capacity, the orphanage could accommodate just less than 400 children and youth. Many teachers willingly donated their time, so we set up a Hebrew school and began circumcising the boys, many of whom had not been circumcised because of their circumstances during the war. Most of the kids adjusted well and settled comfortably into the new environment. Every now and then, however, we had a very wild one—a kid who had acquired some rough edges as a result of what they had to do to survive. Once shown love and care, however, they would become kids again. After the Israeli Independence War Armistice, we began shipping groups of children to their new home in Israel. In time, all the children from the Herzl Orphanage moved to Israel and were taken to live on a kibbutz, all arranged by the Israelis.

One of the highlights of that era was the visit by the mayor of New York City. Mayor Fiorella LaGuardia was visiting American troops stationed in Berlin and when he heard about our orphanage project, he volunteered to be the master of ceremonies for the official opening. Perhaps he knew a great political move and photo opportunity when he saw one. He came with his entourage and gave a speech surrounded by newspaper reporters, cameras, and his own film crew.

When we needed projectors for the small movie theatre we'd set up, I discovered a place on Liebknecht Street in the Russian zone where people were making projectors. I also found out that they had an inventory of portable projectors. One could fold them up and take along. So, one afternoon, I put on my Russian uniform, found myself a chauffeur and drove to the checkpoint border crossing leading to the Russian sector of Berlin. In retrospect, perhaps I should have been more concerned about my safety because, as previously mentioned, if any of the Russians identified me, I would have been shot immediately. To them, I was a deserter, a defector, and a thief who had stolen Russian Air Force property, a saboteur, and of course a traitor. The thought of being captured by the Russians did give me some concern. The orphanage, however, needed projectors and that was all there was to it. I simply had to get my hands on some projectors. As I approached the checkpoint, the Russian border guards simply looked at my uniform and waved the car through. Americans and Russians were allies after all and thank goodness for that. My Russian uniform had opened the door for me.

At the factory on Liebknecht Street, I explained to the manager that I needed some projectors for my air force outfit and fabricated a location. He said I would need a requisition order from headquarters and refused me the two projectors. Then I offered to purchase them and took out a sizable amount of currency from my pocket. Not only was he not tempted by offer, but he also was becoming more and more nervous. In fact, he was shaking. I swear that I could hear his knees knocking together. His nervousness puzzled me a bit. Was it because I was in a Russian Army uniform?

"Okay, you won't give me the projectors; you refuse to sell me the projectors, so this is what I am going to do. While I take two projectors, you go ahead and call your security or whatever…" and I placed my hand on my holstered gun. Looking even more worried, he said: "I don't see anything, I'm not hearing anything, and I'm not here." He turned and left the factory floor. I followed him outside and called my driver to assist me. I knew exactly what was needed. We took two projectors, two projection lamps, two stands, and a screen, loaded them into the car, and headed back to the American sector of occupied Berlin. The orphanage now had a working movie theatre.

To conclude the story of the movie projectors: once all the children were in Israel and the orphanage closed, I was sent to Munich. I took those projectors with me, and they followed me everywhere I went, eventually coming with me to Canada. In the seventies, while I was working at Ottawa University in Ontario Canada, the university's Hindu club wanted to show movies. The university had only 35mm projectors and they needed 16mm projectors, so I offered mine. The university paid me $5,000 for those two projectors. I installed them and as far as I know, they remain in use at Ottawa University to this day.

Head Nurse Clara Winters

Reverand Rotendorf

Dr. Fishbain

New York Mayor Fiorello La Guardia at opening ceremony of the Herzl Orphanage

Head Nurse Clara Winters cuts the ribbon at Herzl Orphanage

The rambling building housing the Herzl Orphanage

Joseph Halpern sets up film projectors

CHAPTER 32

Your Future Country Needs You

In mid-April 1948, I was asleep one night at the DP camp in Berlin when I was awakened during the middle of the night by three young men. These deeply committed and extremely motivated young Jewish men were members of the *Haganah* which was the former paramilitary organization of the Jewish population *Yishuv* in Palestine between 1920 and 1948, when it became the core of the Israel Defense Forces (IDF). It was basically the Jewish Settlement Police from all over Palestine. The *Haganah* would develop into the *Mossad* formed December 13, 1949. At this time the *Haganah* was recruiting pilots and volunteers from all over the world.

One of them asked me, "Do you speak Hebrew?"

"Of course," I replied and continued, "I went to Hebrew school and my grandfather was a rabbi."

"Do you believe in the Jewish State?" He asked. I answered unequivocally, "Of course."

Another of the triumvirate then stated quite emphatically: "The future Jewish State—your future country, Israel, needs you!"

Shortly thereafter, I was escorted out of Berlin and smuggled to Rome. The four of us travelled by car, by truck, and by train—sometimes hidden and sometimes quite openly. I couldn't help but feel rather important. It was as if these three members of the *Haganah* were my personal bodyguards, and they treated me like a high-ranking official whose safety was a top priority. A few days later after leaving Berlin we arrived in Rome.

In February 1947, Britain announced its intention to terminate any involvement in Palestine effective May 15, 1948. This included all militia, governing, and policing. Subsequently, the United Nations General Assembly adopted *Resolution 181*: Effective November 29, 1947, this was the partition plan that would divide Palestine into two separate states (Jewish-Israel and Arab-Palestine), while keeping Jerusalem a UN-controlled international zone. The votes were: 33 for, 13 against, and 10 abstentions. The Jews accepted this result with jubilant celebration. The Arabs, however, rejected it and launched a war of annihilation against the Jewish State. The Arabs threatened to inflict more pain and suffering onto the Jews than Hitler ever had. This declaration galvanized the Jews, while adopting a fight to the death attitude. The Jews were not going to allow another Holocaust!

Since the UN vote for partition, a form of civil war developed between the Jews and the Arabs in Palestine. The rise of deadly incidents was escalating exponentially. Arab forces perpetrated sporadic ambushes and attacks on Jewish targets, mostly to cut off the highway linking Tel Aviv to Jerusalem. The Arabs controlled several strategic vantage points along the route. One of these was a city called Deir Yassin. This city had strategic importance because of its high elevation with a commanding view of the region and its closeness to Jerusalem.

On April 9, 1948, Deir Yassin was attacked by about 130 far-right Jewish militants. Approximately 100 of the village of 700 were slaughtered, mostly women and children. This massacre happened despite the Arabs signing a non-aggression pact with the Jews. As a result, a mass exodus of Palestinians began, while Zionists increased their efforts to promote Jewish immigration.

David Ben-Gurion, head of the Jewish Agency and later Israel's first prime minister, condemned the attack and sent a letter of apology and condemnation to Jordanian King Abdullah. Regardless, the Arabs would soon retaliate.

Some of the groups involved in the *Deir Yassin massacre* were the *Irgun* (a Jewish Zionist paramilitary organization led by Menachem Begin who later became the sixth prime minister of Israel) and the *Lehi* which was the National Military Organization in the Land of Israel. The *Irgun*, which was responsible for the previous bombing of the King David Hotel July

22, 1946, had been formed in 1931 and disbanded in 1948. The Lehi, or "Fighters for the Freedom of Israel," founded in 1940, by Avraham Stern, was also disbanded in 1948.

On April 13, 1948 the Hadassah Medical Convoy Massacre occurred when a convoy escorted by *Haganah* militia, was carrying supplies and personnel to the Hadassah Medical Centre on Mount Scopus, Jerusalem. This convoy was ambushed by Arab forces; 78 were killed, including doctors, nurses, nursing students, patients, faculty members, *Haganah* fighters, and one British soldier. There would be a constant occurrence of massacres perpetrated by both sides right up to the start of the war.

The Hadassah Convoy Massacre

Ben-Gurion knew that the Arabs would attack the newly-formed state of Israel and in order to have a chance of winning this forthcoming war against the Arabs, Israel would need weapons, ammunition, airplanes, and military vehicles. He flew to the United States to meet personally with President Harry S. Truman. Ben-Gurion figured that the USA would graciously supply Israel with a profusion of weaponry, especially considering the abundance of surplus weapons, ammunition, airplanes, and military vehicles left over from World War II. Unfortunately, President Truman firmly believed that Israel had virtually no chance of winning the war with the Arabs, considering that the Jews were outnumbered 50 million to

600,000. Because of this conviction, Truman flat out rejected any offering of exportation of American war surplus to Israel. Also, if that wasn't enough of a slap on the face, not only did Truman refuse to assist Israel, he also was instrumental in leading a world-wide weapons and supplies embargo on the entire Middle East region. Truman even decreed that any American who assisted Israel in any capacity (including serving militarily) would mean the revoking of US citizenship and possible jail time. Fortunately, many Americans ignored these warnings and helped Israel by volunteering as soldiers, pilots, weapon smugglers, and maintenance support, and by donating funds and raising money to pay for all that.

The network by which funds were collected and distributed via the *Haganah* had been set up since 1945. On a previous trip to New York City that year, Ben-Gurion met with around 20 affluent Jewish contributors, mostly businessmen. This notable meeting took place at the residence of an oil tycoon named Rudolf Sonneborn. After that, the Sonneborn Institute was initiated. It collected millions of dollars, so that weapons, support materials, and ships could be purchased (mostly illegally and by setting up fictitious foreign and domestic companies) to make their way to Palestine.

One ship purchased, called *President Warfield* was promptly renamed *Exodus 1947*. In France, it picked up around 4,500 Jewish refugees (mostly Holocaust survivors) and transported them to the shores of Palestine. In the movie "Exodus," starring Paul Newman, the refugees arrived safely in Palestine. Unlike in the movie, the *Exodus 1947 was* attacked by five British destroyers and one cruiser. The British opened fire, threw gas bombs, and rammed the *Exodus 1947* in three directions. Although the refugee passengers had prepared by training and simulating attacks, the ship was boarded with British Royal Marines; a three-hour battle ensued and eventually the Brits took control of the vessel. *Exodus 1947* sustained so much damage during the ordeal that it had to be towed to Haifa, where the refugees were transferred to cargo ships. Under deplorable conditions, they first sailed to Port-De-Bouc, France where the French government would accept the immigrant passengers only if they would debark the ship willingly. The immigrants refused and went on a 24-day hunger strike. This brought worldwide attention to the issue, putting pressure on the British to solve the problem. The Brits decided to send the passengers to DP camps in Germany—a move that was criticized internationally. In time, the vast majority of these refugees would make *Aliyah*, "the act of going up" in Hebrew, which pertains to the act of immigration of Jews to Palestine or Israel and would be in Israel when it was declared a nation.

The Exodus 1947 *transported 4,500 Jewish refugees*

By the peak of the conflict, there were about 3,500 volunteers from 37 countries called *Machal* (Mitnadvei Chutz-La'Arets)—Hebrew for overseas volunteers. Many were not Jewish. Thankfully, and somewhat miraculously, one country was willing to sell weapons, ammunition, and war planes to the Jews. Without Czechoslovakia's help, Israel never would have won this war.

At this time, Rome was the headquarters for the *Haganah* and pilot volunteers. There I met pilots from all over the world; from Poland, England, South Africa, the United States, and many other countries, including a pilot from Canada. His name was Buzz Beurling and was Canada's most famous hero of World War II. He was also known as "The Falcon of Malta." Beurling earned this nickname by inflicting 27 confirmed kills of Axis airplanes within a fourteen-day span during the battle of that besieged island.

A naturally gifted pilot, he was an expert marksman and fearless in battle. He was awarded the "Distinguished Service Order" and the "Distinguished Flying Cross." He ended up with 31 and 1/2 credited kills—more than any other Canadian. On May 20, 1948, we were all devastated to hear that Buzz Beurling was killed in Rome. While he was testing a Norman plane, it burst into flames. Many of us believed that his plane had been sabotaged by Arab spies, possibly even by one of the women who had been hanging around the pilots, but we will never know. After all, Buzz Beurling's presence could have affected the outcome of the entire war. The Arabs would have done anything to prevent this. He was 26.

Gideon Lichtman, an American who was the first pilot to shoot down an enemy plane (the first kill in 1948) and who christened the planes "Messerschitts" to describe the *Avia S-199s,* was supposed to be in the plane that blew up with Beurling in it but had cancelled participation in the doomed flight that morning because he had slept with an Italian girl the night before and they wanted more of each other's company. Instead, an American Leonard Cohen was on the flight with Beurling. Their bodies were burnt beyond recognition.

George Frederick "Buzz" Beurling known as "The Falcon of Malta"

American pilot Gideon Lichtman was first to shoot down an enemy plane

One volunteer, considered to be the founder of the Israeli Air Force, was an American TWA engineer named Al Schwimmer. By utilizing his contacts, organizing abilities, bribery, smuggling, and a whole lot of *chutzpah*, Schwimmer would be instrumental in delivering ten American-built *Curtiss C-46 Commando* transport planes, four American *Boeing B-17* bombers, more than 25 *Avia S-199* fighter planes (refitted *Messerchmitts* manufactured in Czechoslovakia) and 59 British-built *Supermarine Spitfires* to Israel. In order to buy these planes; the *C-46s* and *B-17s* from the US and the *Avia S-199s* and the *Spitfires* from Czechoslovakia, Schwimmer organized and collected millions of dollars from American Zionists.

Frank Sinatra had been entertaining at the Copacabana Night Club in New York City, in the same hotel in which the American headquarters of the *Haganah* was operating from. He became a volunteer himself and offered to collect and distribute funds. Over the years Sinatra would help out the Jewish cause to such an extent that his music and films would be banned in many Arab countries and still are to this day.

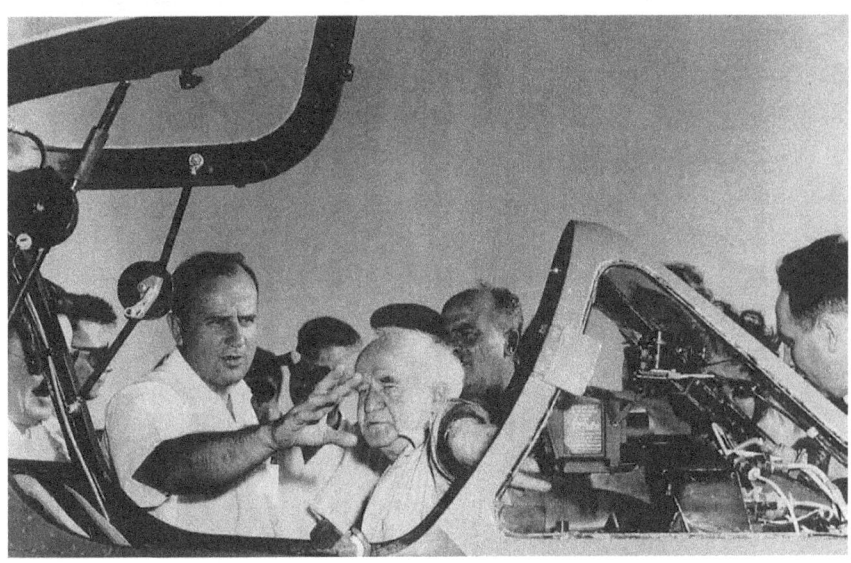

American Al Schwimmer (left) with David Ben-Gurion considered founder of the Israeli Air Force

Schwimmer then had pilot volunteers purchase the *C-46s* from the American war surplus administration in California for USD5,000 each, as US war veterans could do. Schwimmer personally purchased two *B-17* bombers from Charles Winters who was using them to transport freight for his business from Florida to Puerto Rico and two more *B-17* bombers from Donald H. Roberts of Tulsa, Oklahoma for around USD30,000. Although Czechoslovakia was the only country willing to break the embargo and sell weapons and planes to Israel, there was a high cost to pay. The Czechs charged Schwimmer USD180,000 each for the first six *Avia-199s*. This was extremely expensive, especially when factoring in that two of these fighter planes were destroyed in an accident and were never involved in combat. The Jews were desperate and agreed to this outrageous price tag, which at least included weaponry, pilot training, and support materials. In today's currency this would be the equivalent of almost USD2 million for each *Avia S-199*. The *Spitfires* would be purchased in December of 1948 for a cost of USD23,000 each.

After the war, Schwimmer returned to the US to face charges that he had violated the *Neutrality Act,* was convicted, stripped of many rights as an American citizen, fined $10,000 and was kicked out of the US Air Force. Schwimmer and his skills were wanted back in Israel where he founded the Israeli Aerospace Industry. He was awarded the Israel Prize for Life Achievement and Contributions to Israeli Society. Al Schwimmer never asked for a pardon as he felt that he never did anything wrong; regardless, President George W. Bush pardoned Schwimmer on December 23, 2008.

Al Schwimmer had to find a way to get the *C-46* transport planes out of the United States, because of the embargo and the *Neutrality Act*. They couldn't be delivered yet to Palestine as the British were still there enforcing the embargo and on high alert for arms smuggling. Through deals and payoffs, these planes hopscotched around the planet. The *C-46s* were flown by American volunteer pilots, starting from California to Panama, from Panama to Natal, Brazil, from Natal to Casablanca, from Casablanca to Rome, and eventually on to the recently established Jewish air base České Budějovice, Czechoslovakia. The bombers would arrive later on in July via a different route starting out from Florida to San Juan, Puerto Rico to Santa Maria, Azores, to České and on to Israel.

The *Avia S-199* was created in Czechoslovakia. During World War II the Germans built airplane manufacturing facilities for the Luftwaffe in Czechoslovakia. After World War II, the Czechs kept those facilities opened and manufactured more planes. When the request to purchase fighter planes came from Al Schwimmer, the warehouse part of the factory that built the motors for the *Messerschmitt BF-109s* had been destroyed. No *Daimler-Benz DB 605 Messerschmitt* engines were available, so the Czech engineers built the *Avia S-199s* with Messerschmitts chasses, and by installing engines built for *Junkers Jumo 211F* bombers and propellers built for the *Heinkel HE 2* bombers. Later in life, every time I watched the TV show "MacGyver," I thought about the *Avia S-199*, or as we called it the *Mezek* (which means mule in English) or, more eloquently, as Gideon Lichtman nicknamed it the "Messerchitt."

Pilots called the jerry-rigged Avia S-199 *"Messerchitts."*

On May 14, 1948—just as the British mandate in Palestine was set to expire—David Ben-Gurion proclaimed the establishment of the state of Israel. That same day United States President Harry S. Truman recognized the new state of Israel. Immediately, five Arab nations (Egypt, Transjordan, Syria, Lebanon, and Iraq) declared war on Israel.

It was time to get the fighter planes to Israel. The *Avia S-199s* were disassembled and transported from Czechoslovakia along with machine guns, ammunition, and pilots (who slept on the wings) on board the *C-46s* transport planes. Shortly after, I flew my Russian *Yak-9* to Israel.

The Yakovlev Yak-9

My immediate impression of Israel was that it was way too damn hot! I found it difficult to breathe during the day; mercifully, it was better at night. I saw groups of fighters dressed in civilian clothes and uniformed soldiers from the *Haganah*. The distinct colour of the triangular emblem on their shoulder indicated where they came from. Only four of the first six *Avia S-199s* planes were delivered to Israel and still unassembled. Before I arrived, that was the entire Israeli air fighter force.

While assembling the *S-199s* in one hangar at Ekron (later to become the "Tel Nof Israeli Air Force Base), the Egyptians bombed the hangar directly beside it. The entire outcome of the war could be attributed to that one piece of luck. Had that Egyptian plane bombed the hangar with the *S-199s* in it, Tel Aviv would have fallen and there would most likely be no Israel.

The plan at first was to use the *Avia S-199* fighter planes against an Egyptian air base in El Arish; however, in the afternoon of day one (just as the assembling of the planes was nearly complete on May 29, 1948), Shimon Avidan, the Givati Brigade commander of the Israeli Defence Forces (IDF), informed the group that "the entire Egyptian army with 10,000 soldiers was less than 50 kilometres away from Tel Aviv and, if you don't go now, they will be there by morning and there will no longer be an Israel!"

Immediately upon completing the reassembling of the four *Avia S-199s*, having no time for test flights, a group of four pilots rose to the occasion. This group consisted of an American Lou Lenart, who led the mission; a South African Eddie Cohen; and two fighter pilots from Israel. One was Ezner Weizmann (who would become the future commander of the Israeli Air Force and the seventh president of Israel) and the other Israeli pilot was Modi Alon. Alon would end up commanding the revered 101 Israeli Air Force Squadron when it was formed. Eddie Cohen was killed on this mission.

The four pilots alone came face to face with thousands of Egyptian troops consisting of seven infantry battalions, 600 vehicles, and lethal antiaircraft weapons. Lou Lenart made some direct hits and landed a 70-kilogram bomb onto a mass concentration of trucks and troops. While taking ferocious antiaircraft fire, Modi Alon and Ezner Weizman hit some targets successfully as well. Eddie Cohen was immediately out of the battle. Either he was hit by anti-aircraft fire right away or he shot off his own propellers as did occur on occasion because the synchronization between the machine gun firing and the propeller rotation sometimes was off on the refitted *Avia S-199 Messerschmitts*. Either way it was a deeply heartfelt loss.

When all was said and done, (and considering the size of the Arab army), the quartet did not manage a lot of damage on the Egyptians. However, the shock of being attacked by what they perceived as *Messerschmitt BF-109s* fighter planes with the Star of David on the side was overwhelming to the Egyptians and they were driven into chaos. They feared that this was just the tip of the iceberg of Israeli air fighters and that they would be further attacked. Israeli intelligence intercepted a communiqué from the Egyptian commander to Cairo that said: "We were heavily attacked by enemy aircraft and we are scattering." Sometimes, when I think about this, I smile to myself and imagine Hitler rolling over in his grave because—by some kind of miraculous irony—the state of Israel and the fate of the future history of the Jews were saved by only four pilots of the newly-formed Israeli Air Force, of all things, in *Nazi* war planes with the Star of David on them.

American Lou Lenart led the mission

Israeli Modi Alon (with sunglasses) the 101 Squadron's first commander

Ezer Weizsman commanded the Israeli Air Force

South African volunteer fighter pilot Eddie Cohen crashed and burned

At dawn the very next day, two of the remaining three *Avia S-199s* were flown on another mission—this time piloted by Ezer Weizman and an American volunteer named Milton Rubenfeld (who is included on the list of the first five pilot volunteers and who would later have a son named Paul in 1952). His son, Paul Rubenfeld later shortened his name to Paul Rubens and went on to become the actor best known as "Pee Wee Herman." Milton Rubenfeld, like so many of us pilots absolutely loved to fly. After World War II, no American airlines were hiring Jewish pilots so, when asked by the *Haganah* if he would be willing to fly for Israel, he jumped at the opportunity. He immediately called four of his friends in similar circumstances and they all eagerly said yes.

This mission was hugely successful. Just the two of them managed to halt the Jordanian-Iraqi attack from the north. Rubenfeld's *S-199* was hit by ground fire and he had to bail out. Seriously injured, when he hit the ground began getting attacked by Israeli citizens as none knew that the Israelis had fighter planes and thought he was the enemy. Rubenfeld didn't speak Hebrew, yet he managed to halt the attackers by shouting out the names of Jewish foods like *matzah* and *gefilta fish*.

Milton Rubenfeld one of the five founding pilots of the Israeli Air Force

Only one *Avia S-199* remained; on June 3, 1948 Modi Alon, flying solo in it, intercepted a pair of Egyptian *REAF C-47* bombers escorted by four Egyptian piloted *Spitfire* fighter planes over Tel Aviv. As thousands of astonished Israelis looked on, Alon evaded the *Spitfires* and blew the bombers out of the sky. He scored the first air to air bomber kill and instantly became a hero. This propelled him into becoming the 101 Squadron's new commander.

Before being named so, all of the pilots from 101 Squadron were called to a meeting by Modi Alon who wanted to give the squadron a number and insignia. When asked what number, Alon said 101 because he wanted the Arabs to think we had 101 squadrons. Gideon Lichtman came up with the name *Malachi Hamavet* (Angel of Death). Two pilots—Bob Vickman and Stan Andrews, Americans who met studying art at UCLA, California—grabbed a napkin and drew the image of a skull with angel wings wearing a flight helmet and goggles. Both Bob Vickman and Stan Andrews went MIA (Missing in Action) in this war. On October 16, 1948, Modi Alon had previously made plans with his three-month pregnant wife Mina, so he scheduled two morning missions to free up the afternoon. He was killed at the end of the second mission as there was smoke coming from his engine at time of decent, his plane crash landed short of the runway and exploded. It was a demoralizing moment for all of us. The "Angel of Death" insignia is still used on Israeli fighter planes to this day.

Insignia of the 101 Squadron

Although the *Avia S-199* had a devastating effect on the Arabs, and more and more volunteers for Israel were arriving and being trained every day, the sheer numbers of Arabs were starting to surround Israeli strongholds. Fearing Israel's imminent defeat, the UN ordered a cease fire which began on June 11, 1948. The first phase of the war ended positively in some ways for the Jews. The Egyptians had been stopped from the south, the Jordanian-Iraqi forces neutralized in the North, and the Jewish State of Israel was still standing. Peaceful settlements, however, could not be reached and the ceasefire was not extended, ending July 9. A few days after the truce was over on July 15th, three of the American *Boeing B-17* bombers left České for Israel. On route they flew over Cairo. The radio went off from the air traffic control at Cairo Airport, asking the plane to identify itself. An American flying one of the bombers, a former TWA pilot said "Oh, this is TWA Flight 38." The airport crew actually turned on the runway lights for them just as the *B-17s* began dropping their bombs. One of the bombs fell near to King Farouk's palace. This really shook up the Egyptians psychologically, and the next day thousands left the city.

The Israelis were much more determined and organized than the Arabs during the ceasefire and used this time wisely to resupply weaponry and ammunition and to reorganize the troops. The Israelis purchased more fighter planes and now had bombers; they trained more new volunteers; and prepared extremely well all aspects of their strategies. The Arabs on the other hand, even though they had just recently formed the first "Arab League" and declared their own independence from colonial power, seemed more concerned about their individual countries rather than acting as a fully unified front. As a result, Israel went on the offensive after the truce and won most of the strategic battles, cleared the Arabs out of many territories, captured much ground, and finally surrounded the Egyptian army which was concentrated in the Gaza Strip. The Arabs called for an Armistice. The UN forced a ceasefire on January 7, 1949 and when the war was officially declared over on March 10th, Israel controlled 78 per cent of the area (much more than was included in the original partition plan). Approximately 700,000 Arabs who were displaced from their homes, neighbourhoods, and villages became refugees. Since the 1948 Israeli-Arab War, May 14 is known as *Nakba Day* (Arab for day of the catastrophe); on this anniversary the Palestinians remember the confiscation of their property, the collapse of their society, and the loss of their homeland. At the time, I thought to myself, "They started it; we finished it."

The flying force of the 101 Squadron

My first mission was to take-out machine-gun nests and enemy convoys in and around Latrun. The Arabs had taken control of the fort at Latrun, taking advantage of its strategic position around the road to Jerusalem. Arab legionnaires shelled Israeli vehicles traveling on that road, thus effectively imposing a military siege on Jerusalem. No supplies were getting through the blockade.

On my very first day of combat, I ran into—of all things—a *Messerschmitt Bf-109*. Some former German pilots had gotten out of Germany with their planes and ended up fighting for the Arabs. Now, I was fighting Germans again!

In the mornings, I would fly through the mountains, searching for enemy machine-gun nests and convoys. Once I spotted them, I would take them out by utilizing the Yak-9's 20mm *ShVAK*, cannon with 120 rounds that was fired through the aircraft's hollow propeller shaft, and the two 12.7 mm *Berenzin UB* machine guns with 340 rounds; along with dropping grenades. I provided reconnaissance and air support for the 7th Armored Brigade and the Alexandroni Brigade's attack on the Latrun fort. It was unsuccessful, and we sustained many casualties.

A second attack on the fort took place on June 1, codenamed *Ben Nun Bet*. Although we took out a lot of their defenses, and I personally shot up and blew up many strategic targets, the operation was also not that successful. So, I kept on with my routine: fly in the morning; find a machine gun nest and take it out; find an enemy convoy; take it out. I was also kept busy checking the planes, preparing arms and ammunition, and training new volunteers.

Meanwhile, in order to circumvent the blocked road, the resourceful Israelis constructed a makeshift camouflaged roadway through the seemingly unsurpassable mountains. This road bypassed the main routes overlooking Latrun and was named the "Burma Road" after the emergency supply route constructed between Kunming, China and Lashio, Burma by the Allies in World War II. On June 9, 1948, the first supplies got through to Jerusalem, putting an end to the month-old Arab blockade.

I continued to keep the roadway free so that supplies could be brought to Jerusalem and other Israeli army units. That became my main mission plus providing air support to many of the battles that ensued. Every now and then, I would end up in a dog fight with a German Messerschmitt, and I was always happy to be able to kill more Germans. That's the way my time in the Israeli Air Force went until the UN sanctioned ceasefire on March 10, 1949.

After the defeat of the Arabs and during the Armistice that ensued, the Israeli commanders asked me if I wanted to stay on. They all hoped that I would remain in Israel and promised me a fulfilling and aspiring career in the Israeli Air Force. I thanked them for the offer but explained to them that I could not handle the hot weather and graciously declined. They made arrangements to have me sent back to Berlin.

Upon arriving back in Berlin, my orphanage was in full bloom. We developed a plan to send most of those parentless kids to the new state of Israel. I knew that they were going to be well cared for and that gave me a comforting feeling. I will always vividly remember watching new Jewish refugees filled with immense bliss immediately kissing the earth after landing on Israeli soil. Having played a significant part in creating the Israeli Air Force and saving the state of Israel, I will always feel a sense of pride and joy because of it.

CHAPTER 33
Time to Leave Berlin

One morning, I was called into the office of the American UNRA (the United Nation Relief Association). UNRA staff managed the displaced persons' camps as part of the occupational forces. I was told by my curator, the person responsible for me, that the Russians (the NKVD), had been snooping around asking questions. Looking over at me he said: "It's getting too hot...time to leave Berlin." His expression was one of concern, and he added, "As soon as possible!"

That day I packed my clothes, books, photos, some trinkets, my medals and the projectors into a crate; Sophie had even fewer items. Money was not a concern. I was issued a Can-Carte. The Can-Carte stated that we were under the jurisdiction of the UNRA and that we were entitled to all types of assistance from the organizations involved. With a Can-Carte, one had free transportation on the underground, trains, and buses within the American, French, and English sectors of Berlin. We were not allowed, however, to enter the Russian sector. (I had, of course, at the risk of immediate death, already entered Russian territory on two occasions—once to get Sophie out and another time to get the movie projectors). The Can-Carte had our name, date of birth, height, weight, hair, and eye colour. UNRA had found us a flight to Munich and we arrived that same evening. UNRA then provided us accommodation in another survivor camp.

Shortly after, I was told to help myself to dwelling in any villa I could find. Sophie and I found a large villa that had been the home of some Gestapo big shot. The villa had two levels, and we moved into the ground level. It came with two bedrooms for us, a living room, and a kitchen—plus a groundskeeper and a housekeeper, both living upstairs.

With no money problems and comfortable accommodation, I enrolled at Munich University, where I doubled the usual workload and thus managed to earn my degrees fast—eventually graduating with a doctorate in electrical engineering. I used what little spare time I had learning about sound engineering and the filmmaking business. Through my associations with the university, I became acquainted with a man who had been a Polish film director before the war. This was just a hobby for me, but I learned a lot about film, set lighting, and sound recording.

Sophie occupied herself attending many social clubs, learning German, and joining several arts and crafts clubs. Sophie and I still maintained a platonic relationship and slept in separate quarters throughout the time we spent in Germany after the war. It would not be until we came to Canada that we decided to become a couple. We ended up staying in Munich for almost four years.

During that after-war period, Jewish survivors mostly wanted to get out of Germany, including me. Many countries were accepting these survivors through immigration programs. Most countries had a quota on the number of immigrants allowed. Sophie and I eventually were offered a spot in Bolivia. So now I was on the way to becoming a citizen of South America. "Well," I thought when I found this out, "at least I will be out of Germany." This was a very positive thing and essential to my long-term safety and survival.

Joseph Halpern working on his doctorate in Munich

CHAPTER 34

"I Still Won't Eat Oranges"

In order to migrate to Bolivia, Sophie and I had to meet certain prerequisites. Each of us had to prove that we could be self-sufficient instead of becoming a burden on Bolivian society. This process went rather well, as I had my doctorate degree and Sophie was a nurse. A few weeks later, and after a complete medical examination and tests, we were cleared to board the ship. The UNRA scheduled a sailing date for us to Bolivia in early February, 1952. One month before that, we were sent to a quarantine camp in Bremerhaven, a German port city, where we would wait out the required month period of quarantine and then set sail from that port.

The Port of Bremerhaven where Joseph and Sophie quarantined

Approximately 60 of us, mostly couples, lived in quarantine in a small section cordoned off by roadblocks. It was actually quite well organized. Couples or small single groups of two or three people were provided small houses in which to live during the quarantine process. It was as if we were our own little village. Sophie and I were assigned to a small house a few doors down from the mess hall building, where we ate breakfast, lunch, and supper. This mess hall also served as the administration office and as a social centre.

The mess was well-equipped with a library, radio, puzzles, cards, board games, and other pastimes. Some would-be immigrants passed the time by playing cards, chess, and board games while some just sat reading or listening to the radio all day. Several women worked preparing food in the kitchen just to pass the time. These women usually were rewarded with an orange. Although a movie was shown every couple of days, the number of films available was limited, and each movie was shown over and over.

Both Sophie and I found it extremely boring. About three weeks into the quarantine, we heard an announcement over the PA system saying that a transport was leaving for Canada that very day. A couple scheduled to leave on that transport had become ill. Now there was an opening; any husband and wife wishing to take their place should report to the office. Sophie was playing cards with a small group of women, and I was sitting in an armchair reading when we heard the announcement. Immediately, I stood up and said to Sophie, "Let's go!" She nodded yes, placing her playing cards on the table. We hurried towards the office; we wanted to be the first ones there. Not only were we the first ones, we were also the only ones.

It had taken more than three months to prove that we were healthy enough and potentially self-sufficient in order to receive the papers required to immigrate to Bolivia; it took less than 10 minutes to process us for Canada. We had been travelling on Non-Citizen, German-issued passports with an exit-immigration visa to Bolivia. The office provided each of us a brand-new exit-immigration visa to Canada. Armed with our fresh documents, we returned to our small house, packed quickly, and went to the port. As instructed, we left our baggage crate at our house, as it would be picked up and loaded on the ship for us. When we boarded the boat, I had no hand luggage and Sophie carried only a small handbag. In the morning, we had been passing the time in quarantine and now were en route to a new life in

Canada. While boarding the *MS Anna Salén*, I thought to myself "Oh, what the hell…." I turned and waved good-bye to Germany.

Our ship already had acquired some history. She had been built in Pennsylvania in 1939 and named the *Mormacland*. She had been designed as a cargo vessel that could handle almost 12,000 tons. She was about 500 feet in length and almost 70 feet wide at centre. But in 1940, before completion, she was taken over by the US Navy and refitted as an aircraft carrier. In 1941, the British Royal Navy commissioned her as the *HMS Archer* for use as convoy protection during the war. She then collided with and actually sank the American ship *SS Brazos* in early 1942 and was so badly damaged that she had to be towed back to Pennsylvania.

In 1945, after the war, the Ministry of War Transport took her over and renamed her yet again. Once more she had been refitted to her original designation as a cargo ship. Then she was returned to US Maritime Commission a year later as the *Empire Lagan*. Then Sven Salén of Stockholm purchased her, rebuilt her as a passenger ship, and named her the *MS Anna Salén*. By the time we boarded her, she had already transported thousands of immigrants to their new homes. After our sailing, the *Anna Salén* was to be renamed three more times until she was scrapped back at home in the United States in the early sixties.

The MS Anna Salén *brought Joseph and Sophie to Canada*

Sophie and I had separate quarters; each room had a shower, a toilet, a small dresser, and a cot-like sleeping bed attached to the wall. We boarded in the late morning, and the ship started to sail towards the English Channel at around four in the afternoon. Sophie and I stood on deck of the boat near the bow leaning against the rail. As soon as the ship began to move, I became seasick. I remember thinking how strange this was. From the time that I had begun flying in gliders to flying fighter planes at hundreds of kilometers per hour in thousands of different positions—up and down, upside down, and sideways (and even during training in the centrifuge), I had never felt even remotely sick. Yet somehow, the slow back-and-forth rocking motion of the ship rendered me completely incapacitated. I needed to lie down.

I didn't vomit, though. If I laid flat on my back, I still felt nauseous but not as much as when I attempted to be vertical. All I could do was read. I spent quite a lot of time looking through Canadian department store catalogues such as Sears and Hudson Bay. I was a bit in awe of the magnitude of merchandise available through those catalogues, especially when I saw that one could even order a house. Not knowing the exact currency exchange, I was left with the impression that things in Canada were very inexpensive. A feeling of gladness came over me at that moment as I thought that Canada was going to be a good place to live.

I had no appetite whatsoever; however, I knew that I needed some sustenance, so I let my training take over and I forced myself to eat. Oranges were all that I could manage to keep in my stomach. For 10 days and nights, I remained in that condition—reading and living on oranges. Adding to my dismay was the fact that I heard that the food on the ship was excellent. I suppose that, in my weakened state, I was feeling a bit sorry for myself. Uncharacteristically, I experienced some feelings of jealousy and of anger. I also felt a tad left out as I could not enjoy all the great food Sophie was telling me about.

Once a day the ship doctor visited me and encouraged me to get out of my chambers and onto the deck, saying that I needed to get some fresh air in order to feel better. Every day I would go up on the deck—and feel even worse. I would remain on the deck for quite a while (or until the doctor was out of range) and then make my way back to my room eager to be horizontal on my cot. And so, it went—every day a fight with the doctor, every day out on the deck feeling worse, and eventually sneaking back to my quarters where I could somehow manage the situation. This is how it went except for one night. During the eighth night, while we were in the mid-east Atlantic, the seas became really rough. The ship was going up and down as if it were riding mountain ranges. As a matter of fact, the captain sent out an SOS that night.

That night I felt great; my appetite was back! I made my way to the kitchen and managed to obtain some beef soup with a few slices of bread from the staff. It was such a relief to feel well again and have an appetite; I felt like I was in heaven. After eating the soup and bread, I went onto the deck. In every direction I saw dozens of people crouching down, holding buckets, lying down being sick, or having just vomited. Some were lying in their own vomit and moaning. I went to one of the public washrooms, gathered up some paper towels, and went from person to person helping them clean themselves up. I brought buckets to some and helped others return to their quarters. Some eventually became well enough to ride out the storm, so to speak, remaining on the deck. Some did not respond to me at all; they just lay there moaning.

Although I spent the rest of the night helping people, I became seasick again the next morning when the seas became calmer. Again, I was lying on my back reading and forcing oranges into my system. At the end of our journey across the Atlantic, we arrived at Pier 21 in Halifax on February 9, 1952. For a long time, I could not even look at an orange; to this day, I cannot eat one.

CHAPTER 35

"Oh, Canada"

Shortly after the ship reached Halifax, I began to feel better. Sophie was in my quarters urging me on, and eventually, we left the ship. It was snowing as we made our way to the line forming in front of the immigration office. The line moved incredibly fast, as the paperwork was mere formality—confirming checklists, stamping passports, and so forth. All of us received a yellow card indicating that we were officially Canadian refugees and $10. The Canadian agents were all good-natured, patient, and friendly. I began to wonder if all Canadians were like this. I started to feel at home, developing an immediate affinity with this country.

The Canadian Jewish Congress (CJC) had now taken over. Once processed, Sophie and I were taken to the train station immediately. On the way the driver told us that we would be taking a train to Montreal where arrangements already had been made for us to live.

We boarded the train, sharing a berth this time. Within a few hours, the train left the station and it continued to snow all the while. As a matter of fact, we spent over two days on that train from Halifax to Montreal, with many stops along the way. And each and every time I looked out the window of our berth, all I could see was snow. Not knowing much about Canadian geography or weather, I thought that Canada was like this year-round. I didn't mind that at all as I had always loved the snow and preferred colder weather.

It snowed continuously for over two days. When we finally arrived at the train station in Montreal, no one could pick us up; we were snowed in. Sophie and I spent another night on the train. By the morning, the snow had stopped and eventually the streets were cleared enough so that traffic could move. Around 10 in the morning, taxis began arriving and people started leaving the train.

The taxi brought us to an apartment just off Park Avenue in old Montreal. The CJC had paid for room and board for us with a young Jewish couple who were renting an apartment on the second floor and had a spare room. The young man worked as a sheet-metal presser and the young woman stayed at home. The young couple let us know that this arrangement made between the couple and the CJC could continue for as long as Sophie and I needed.

At that time, Sophie and I were still living platonically. Although we didn't talk about it, I was thinking that it would be best to find a place for us with separate sleeping areas as soon as possible. For now, the situation was more than adequate. I discovered that the CJC knew about my doctorate degree in electronics and that I also had firsthand experience. They lined up a job opportunity for me at RCA Victor in Montreal, and I had a job interview the following week. As I spoke neither French nor English yet, an interpreter accompanied me to that interview. It was like a miracle for me; for the first time in quite a long time, I felt as if I was beginning to have my own life back. It was a feeling of profound comfort and joy. I began work almost immediately.

Now that my near future was secure, I began wondering what had happened to my parents.

After I had arrived at the DP camp in Berlin, I had made every effort to find out about my parents. All my efforts to find out about my parents led to a dead end. During my time in Munich, I had travelled to every Jewish Congress Centre throughout Europe. Jews from all over the world were making lists at these centers. I travelled to practically every country in Europe, and searched those lists relentlessly, with hope, anticipation, and unmitigated effort. Each time, after looking through another list, I would despairingly leave my name on it and then muster up more optimism so that I had the energy to continue searching. Once I heard that someone caught word that my parents had survived and were in Australia.

I took every transport I could—trucks, trains, ships, and planes—to get to Australia. I spent weeks there checking lists and asking around in the major cities. It was of no consequence; always it was the same story—one dead end after another.

Sophie and I had been in Montreal for a couple of weeks, and things were looking quite good. We had comfortable lodgings and I had a job. One evening I was sharing my tales of my international search for my parents with the young couple we were living with. The young man told me about the Canadian Jewish Centre just a few blocks away, saying that it had many lists there. Sophie and I agreed that I should go down there right away.

"I'll go there tomorrow first thing after breakfast." I said to Sophie. With hopefulness, I added, "Will you go with me?"

"Of course, I'll go with you!" she answered, looking surprised that I would even have to ask.

The young man was right. The CJC was nearby, and the next morning we got there in no time at all. Sophie and I walked down the stairs, and I opened the door to let her in ahead of me. The very first person I saw when I walked in was my father! Amidst all kinds of papers with lists stuck to the walls was a desk, and my father was sitting on a chair directly in front of me talking to another man. My father's head turned towards me, and our eyes met. Even though we had not seen each other for almost 11 years, since 1941 in fact, I could see the instant recognition in his eyes.

"Abba!" I exclaimed.

"Joseph!" he answered with exhilaration, rising from his chair. We were soon locked in an embrace, hugging each other and circling the floor as we were in a dance of elation and excitement.

Tears were flowing from both our eyes. Crying seemed easier for him; my tear ducts had not been used for some time. It didn't matter. This time I didn't hold back any emotions.

"You're alive!" he burst out. "Thank God…you're alive!"

I answered, "You, too!" wiping the tears from my eyes as our lock loosened a little.

"Let me look at you! Let me see my son, my only son!" he said.

It turns out that my father had heard that another transport had arrived, and he too had come to the CJC to check the lists. He had been in Canada for a few years by then and, like me, had been checking lists all over the planet. In the following weeks, we both would have hundreds of questions for each other.

"Your mother is alive; she is here in Montreal. We are both here. Now you are here, too. We need to tell her that you're alive!"

After a while my father and I began to settle down a bit. I introduced Sophie to him as my good friend who had travelled from Germany to Canada with me. He hugged Sophie and then turned to me and said, "Come…let's go see your mother. It's a short walk from here." Sophie decided to leave us alone for that reunion and went back to the apartment.

On the way to my parents' place in Montreal, I found out that the very next day after I had left home and reported to that cadet training area, my parents had fled Vladimir Volynsky. With help from one of his brothers and a lot of money, they managed to make their way to England and eventually to Canada.

When we arrived at the apartment building on Hutchison Street, my father suggested that I stay at the bottom of the stairway out of sight. My mother was an intensely emotional woman, so he wanted to break the news about me to her in stages. Otherwise, she might go into some form of shock—or faint, for sure. My father climbed the steps, took out his key to the apartment, unlocked and opened the door. He remained outside and called excitedly for my mother.

"Ethel!" he called out. "Can you please come see me at the door?" I could hear her voice from below the stairs and behind the wall where I was hiding.

"Is there something wrong, Bernard?"

I could visualize the smile on his face as he spoke. "No, nothing is wrong. As a matter of fact, I have some good news to share with you— some very good news.

"What is it?" As my mother spoke, I was doing my best to contain myself. I wanted to run up those stairs, see her, and hug her!

"It's about Joseph!"

"What good news about Joseph?" I could hear the excitement rising with each syllable in her voice.

"He's alive!" my father told her. "He survived!"

My mother was now very close to the door and asked my father, "How do you know this?"

My father answered with unmistakable exhilaration in his voice and tears of joy in his eyes. "Because he's here!" My father then called for me to come up the stairs. Halfway up the stairs, my mother appeared through the door. I hesitated for a split second then felt a surge of pure love enveloping me as I continued my ascent.

My mother fell to her knees and reached to me while she lovingly called my name "Joseph! Joseph! Joseph!" She just kept repeating my name. I reached out my arms near the top of the stairs, met her outstretched arms, and practically lifted her into the air.

"Ima!" I shouted with the purest joy that I had ever experienced. As we embraced in the way only a mother and son can, I realized that this time I was actually really crying.

Later, that day my father would share with me that, because the Jewish population had been so decimated, it was my duty as a Jewish survivor to produce as many children as possible. He encouraged me to change my relationship with Sophie, make a new life for myself in Canada, and produce children.

In the following years, I listened to my father's advice, married Sophie and fathered five children: David, George, Anna-Lee, Leo, and Saul.

Joseph's father Bernard Halpern

Joseph's mother Ethel Halpern

AFTERWORD

After arriving in Canada in 1952 Dad immediately began working for RCA Victor in Montreal. At RCA he became known as the "goodbye guy." On his first day on the job, not yet fluent in English, he greeted his new fellow workers with a confident "goodbye!" Mom and Dad moved into their own apartment, and my brother David was born in July 1953.

Dad was soon transferred to the Ottawa office of RCA and shortly afterward purchased a house on Corbeil Street in Hull (now Gatineau), Quebec, a town just across the river from Ottawa, where the main industry at that time was the E.B. Eddy pulp and paper. The houses in Hull were less expensive than in Ottawa and the Quebec Government was providing financial incentives to buy homes there. This was the house where I grew up after being born in 1955.

At the "Corbeil House," as it would to be called, Dad started a flourishing TV repair business in our basement, where he created and maintained an amazing workshop. He achieved this in partnership with another RCA Victor technician. They both kept their day jobs at RCA Victor and ran their own business after work and on weekends. My dad's partner's name was Lou Lamoreaux and their business thrived.

Lamoreaux would do the home visits because his French and English were better. He would simply determine if it was a problem with the picture tube or not. If not the picture tube, he would remove the chassis from the TV, disconnect the picture tube, and deliver the chassis to Dad. Dad would then repair any problem with the workings in the chassis. Dad manufactured a unique adaptor that would allow any chassis to connect with his test picture tube. Once repaired Lamoreaux would redeliver the chassis and reconnect the picture tube. Sometimes Lamoreaux would bring Dad the entire TV set. Many a time I carried many a TV up and down the stairs at the side door. (In those days TVs were large and heavy). This enterprise enabled Dad to put his five children through private Hebrew School. Dad lived at the Corbeil House for over three decades.

Due to the loss of so many Jews in the Holocaust, my grandfather's directive to beget as many children as possible constantly reverberated in Dad's thoughts and was his driving motive in having a large family. Dad would have had more than five kids if not for the fact that Mom's mental health was on a downhill spiral. Once in later years, Dad spoke to me in confidence and said that in retrospect, there was always something peculiar about my mother that he just could not put a finger on. That haunting awareness about my mother's nature did manifest itself eventually and turn into something quite ugly for the family when she experienced a psychological breakdown.

At first, other than some paranoid thoughts about the German neighbours across the street being Nazis and occasionally spitting at them, Mom seemed to be managing their new life quite well. Our home was usually the centre of neighbourhood activities, birthday parties, and other neighbourhood gatherings. Mom was becoming quite the socialite and, at first Dad felt comfortable going to work every morning, knowing that Sophie was being a good mother and staying generally well occupied.

One evening, Dad came home with a brand-new car. Mom had expected that the money would be used for something else. An argument ensued, and Mom began angrily hurling dishes at him. In a short while, the entire kitchen floor was littered with broken glass. Mom had managed to smash every breakable object within her reach. David, just eight and me just six years old, were downstairs and in bare feet. Dad had to carry us across the kitchen floor to the bedroom that we shared. Dad attempted to explain to David and me that our mother was just upset, and things would be better soon. Deep down, Dad knew that David and I both had understanding way beyond our years, and we were not taken in by Dad's sugar coating. Anna-Lee and Leo somehow managed to sleep through the ordeal. Saul was not yet born.

From that day things went downhill in our household. One morning I wet my bed. Mom was so angry that she had grabbed me by my hair, lifted me up by my hair, and rubbed my face forcefully in the urine-soaked mattress saying, "If you act like a dog, you will be treated like a dog!" This incident, among others (such as Mom chasing the neighbours' children out of the house brandishing a butcher knife while swearing profusely in Russian) was the turning point in the frustrating procedure of finding professional help for her. It was a classic catch-22: Mother refused medical intervention. Our family doctor, Dr. Morris Resnick, was licensed in Ontario, so he could not come to our home in Quebec in order to have Mom committed. No Quebec doctor could force treatment on Mom, as there were neither local records nor historical precedent to support any action of that kind.

This predicament continued for a few years until one day, my sister Anna-Lee wrote to the *Ottawa Citizen* newspaper to the attention of a columnist similar to Dear Abby. In the letter Anna provided details of enduring knife-wielding threats and existing in a constant state of fear. The story broke on the front page and, within a couple of days, a doctor arrived with two attendants and a van. It amazed all of us just how fast politics could cut through red tape. Sophie Halpern was committed to Pierre Janet Medical Hospital in Hull, where she was diagnosed with paranoid schizophrenia.

Initial treatments helped. While on medication, Mom became somewhat well again. The problem was that Mom could not manage to keep on her medication regime and experienced frequent relapses. Finally, the doctors agreed that the best option was to have her committed to a permanent home. That halfway house was quite a distance north. Dad never visited her. We did not know then that he was developing a relationship with another woman and had no motivation whatsoever to have anything more to do with Mom. I went several times with my own family; it was depressing.

Mom died in 2007 and is buried just outside Montreal. David and I were the only family members who attended Mom's funeral.

Dad endured by sheer force of will and managed to focus on his career. In 1965 Dad was hired by Ottawa University as a research technologist. During his time at Ottawa University, Dad became directly involved with many unique, interesting and sometimes secretive projects. He worked on projects such as the development of the MRI. Dad worked on projects with the Department of National Defense and the Canadian military. He consulted for and received an award from NASA for his work on the guidance system and batteries utilized on the Apollo moon missions. On a lighter note, Dad was working with batteries which he knew were going to be left on the lunar surface so he secretly inscribed His initials JIH in an unseen area on one of the batteries. Yes, Dad's initials remain on the moon.

After the Apollo 11 mission, Ottawa University received some moon rocks to study. For quite some time, Dad had a chunk of one of those moon rocks in his laboratory. Dad always took pleasure and a little pride in showing that rock, especially to me because my eyes lit up with excitement and awe every time I saw that moon rock and held it in my hands.

Dad managed to achieve those milestones while working on and obtaining his second doctoral degree and also taking additional courses in advanced quantum physics. Lingering in the back of his mind was the constant painful awareness of his wife's condition.

I suppose the loss of all Dads' family, with the exception of Grandmother and Grandfather, kept him from opening up to anyone. Dad confided in me when I became an adult and began listening to his many stories that he never really was in love with Mom; their relationship was simply one of convenience. Dad had never actually been truly happy since his childhood and teenage days with Isabelle. That is until he met Heather Pigden.

Heather Pigden when her and Joseph's love affair began

It was at a friendly gathering in May 1969, when Heather and Dad met for the first time. She was 26 years younger than he, had cerebral palsy, and walked with two canes. None of those things mattered to Dad. It was simply "love at first sight." In some ways, Heather shared gestures and mannerisms with Isabelle. Although Heather and Isabelle did not look much alike, sometimes Dad felt as if Heather was the reincarnation of his lost childhood sweetheart. Fortunately, Heather's feelings for Dad were mutual and they began what was to be over 40 years of loving companionship. Dad was once again in love and joy was back in his life.

My father, Joseph Israel Halpern was a kind man. My older daughter Mandy said, "Grampa Zeda was "my hero!" Dad was a hero—as a Russian fighter pilot in World War II, Dad is credited with 22 confirmed planes shot down. As a fighter pilot, Dad was shot down four times. He earned four Red Star medals as a hero to the Soviet Union; he trained as a special commando; was taught how to see in the dark; hear whispers; blend into a crowd and disappear; survive torture, and of course capture and/or kill high-ranking German targets. Dad also flew as a fighter pilot for the new nation of Israel in the 1948 conflict.

Dad was also a loving father, a great scientist, a member of Mensa and one of the funniest guys you could ever know. We Halperns come from a long line of scholars and rabbis. My great-grandfather, Reb Schlomo Halevi Halpern, was a scholar and is legendary in the Jewish community for the creation of a new way of thinking ("meta-learning") for Hebrew scholars. The Warsaw of his day abounded with Jewish learning; with thousands of synagogues and centers for Torah teaching and learning, scholars young and old would fill those centers to study the word of God. At the close of business merchants and artisans would join the crowds in those centers and study into the evening hours. Only a select few could earn the recognition of the community. Rabbi Halpern enjoyed the esteem of those renowned sages and men of wisdom. He was constantly encouraged to spread his teachings and eventually became known as "Reb Schloma'leh Hamalach (translated "Reb Schlomo the angel"). Reb Schlomo traveled by train across Europe and would be greeted at each stop by crowds of eager fans anticipating his arrival. Those fans would listen intently to every word Reb Schlomo would say, often utilizing humor. In a way, he was like a comedian/scholar on tour. My brother David, my late brother Leo, my late brother Saul, and I often joked about what happened to that part of our lineage.

Dad was an only child. My grandfather, however, was one of 12 children. For the first 10 years of Dad's life, my grandfather was serving a 10-year sentence for being a Marxist and my dad with his mother would visit him once a year. When my grandfather eventually came home, there was quite an adjustment to be made within the family.

When Dad was only one year old, the doctors told my grandparents that his brain was about one and a half times normal size. As a curious kid, Dad was the collector in the neighbourhood. He kept bottle caps, screws, bolts—basically anything he found. As his collection increased, he organized these items and soon developed a reputation for having things that people needed. Inevitably, soon enough, if anyone needed something they would seek him out, and that is the foundation of his character and his organization skills.

My father loved to study as well. I suppose watching all the scholars coming to his home in Vladimir Volynsky to meet with, study and debate the Torah with my great-grandfather Reb Schlomo inspired him. Dad obtained two doctorate degrees. One doctorate degree in electrical engineering from Munich University and another PhD in quantum physics at Ottawa University; yet, he was modest about those accomplishments. My brother David did not even know about Dad's second PhD until the week before Dad died. David said to me, "You mean Dad had two PhDs?" Dad also could speak eight languages including Arabic. Of course, he could read Hebrew and Yiddish. What I found amazing is that Dad could read the Koran in its original language. However, despite the fact that languages came easy to him and his English, although spoken with a heavy accent, was excellent, somehow learning French evaded him.

When Dad took up a project, it ended up being amazing. Naturally, stories about our school projects became legendary. I have an early memory of when I was three- or four-years old riding in a foot pedal-powered kiddy car. Of course, dad had modified the kiddy car. He'd painted it metallic green, added blinker lights and a horn.

When I was in grade one at the Hillel Academy during Purim there was the traditional costume contest. Dad made David and me robot costumes out of cardboard boxes which he painted a shiny grey. To each he then added blinking eyes, moving antennas, the standard horn and a control panel about waist high. Of course, David and I shared first prize and were equipped for Halloween for the next few years.

One year during Hebrew school there was a Chanukah menorah building contest. Dad made a beautiful menorah using various sizes of copper tubing. Under each candleholder he constructed a Star of David. Not only did this spectacular work of art win first prize, it was put in the main display case and remained there for over 40 years. At first the principal had a plaque made with Dad's name on it, but in his usual way of avoiding the limelight, Dad asked that his name be removed from the donation credit.

Further along in life when Dad fell in love with Heather, he wrote a love poem for her titled "The Meadow." Sure enough, Dad's poem "The Meadow" ended up being broadcast on CBC Radio. The CBC put music to it, found a professional narrator, and aired the poem several times.

Dad also had a mischievous side to him. One summer day we were so bored that I asked Dad if he could suggest an activity or prank. He seriously suggested that we climb the roof of the Catholic school down the street and set off the warning siren! He began to provide me with instructions how to trigger the siren. It was probably a good thing that I decided against this action.

Gentle as his spirit was, Dad was also extremely physically tough and he didn't like hospitals. An example of his dislike of hospitals is "The Coke Bottle Story." When I was very young, I watched as Dad opened the fridge door and a 26-ounce glass Coca-Cola bottle fell onto his left foot severing the main artery in his toe. The blood shot up like a fountain, gushing blood in the air almost a metre high. I watched as Dad calmly reached for a dish towel, placed the towel at the top of the spewing blood flow and gently pushed the blood stream down until the towel reached his toe. Dad then nonchalantly wrapped the dish towel around his toe and tied it with a knot. By now the dish cloth was soaked with blood so Dad reached for another dish towel, proceeded to knot a secondary wrap, he then put on one shoe and drove to the store. He really wanted a Coke. From that day onward and for the rest of his life, Dad had no mobility in his left toe.

One night dad came home after being t-boned in a car accident. His left bicep muscle was squashed to a point of non-existence and his entire upper arm was completely bruised: at first blue, purple, and black; later yellow and green. Dad of course refused to go to the hospital and lived the rest of his life without a visible bicep muscle on his left arm.

Once the crew from Ottawa RCA Victor put together a broomball team and they all went down to Montreal to compete against the RCA team there. During that game Dad was checked into the boards and injured his right shoulder. Against all the other players' advice, of course, Dad again refused to be taken to the hospital and in fact continued to play out the game. From that moment on until about 50 years later Dad could not move his right arm above his shoulder. I was living with Dad in Ottawa when I was awakened around 3 o'clock in the morning by a loud thud. While sneaking a dark chocolate treat, Dad, then 83 years old had fallen off a stool and landed on his right shoulder. Somehow to our amazement and awe, this ordeal fixed that lingering problem and after that fall, Dad miraculously regained complete motion in his right arm.

Although Dad was a trained commando with the ability to kill with his hands, he controlled his anger with us, but every now and again some incident would trigger Dad's deep-rooted anger and on occasion his training would manifest itself. Because Dad had come close to death so many times in the war, he was living his life as if every day was a bonus and a blessing. He was not prone to survivor guilt. Dad shared with me that he believed he did not have the "fear gene" and could not remember ever actually being afraid. One time in particular, however, he told me that he came close to it.

On an RCA service call, Dad was sent to the Russian embassy in Ottawa. He entered the building with wariness. Once signed in and equipped with a guest pass, Dad was ushered to a room deeper inside the embassy. As soon as he was left alone in that room, he heard the sounds of the doors being locked! He tried the doors and yup, sure enough, they were indeed locked. Dad said out loud "Well Joe...looks like they finally got you." It all ended well as the doors were soon opened, and it turned out to be just routine. At that moment it hit me. Dad was on the KGB wanted list and had to live out his entire life with that awareness in the back of his mind.

One afternoon Dad was driving on Isabelle Street in Hull. As Dad approached the streetlight to turn onto Saint Raymond, a biker was idling his chopper in front of Dad. The biker was wearing a jacket with a swastika painted on back. Dad got out of his car, walked directly up to the biker, and said, "Take off that jacket!" The biker said to Dad "Fuck you!" Dad repeated, "Take off that jacket," then added "or I will rip it off you!" The biker was considerably bigger that Dad and was not at all intimidated by him. The biker then turned off his motorcycle, parked the bike on its stand and began to engage my father in a fight. Dad beat up the biker so badly that he had to be taken away by ambulance. The police were involved, but in those days a report was filed and that was the end of the police activity.

Dad decided to visit this fellow in the hospital. When he arrived, Dad met up with the biker's father, who actually thanked Dad for "knocking some sense into my son." The biker, lying in the hospital bed all bandaged up practically from head to toe apologized to Dad, stating that he had not been aware of the holocaust and what the swastika represented. The biker then promised Dad and his father that he would never again wear a swastika symbol again.

Dad had a unique parenting method. During my high school years Mom was at the peak of her illness and provided little input towards our upbringing. Dad was playing roles both as father and mother. Every night, he would prepare lunches for each of us. In the morning, David and I would catch the local school bus to go to Philemon Wright High School, and Dad would then drive Anna-Lee, Leo and Saul to Hebrew school in Ottawa. The following year Anna-Lee graduated from Hillel Academy and joined David and me attending PWHS. Leo and Saul ended up in public school in Hull.

One evening Dad and I had a heart-to-heart. He told me that I would have a long leash and that I could talk with him about anything and he would not judge. He said that his job was to help me. I could stay out as late as I wanted; as long as he knew where I was and that I was safe. I could take days off school for whatever reason as long as I told Dad.

One day in Grade 10, one of my classmates, Keith Wilson (whose parents were not as liberal minded) approached me before class began in the morning. Keith told me that his parents were forcing him to get a haircut and, if he did not manage that, he could not to come home. His parents of course were bluffing, thinking that Keith would arrive home with his hair clipped. Keith was going to run away from home and hitchhike to Montreal. Keith asked me if I would go with him. I told him that I would have to call my father first.

I called Dad and reached him in his lab at Ottawa University. I explained to Dad that I wanted to go with Keith and watch out for him. Dad asked me if we wanted to come by the university first and get some money from him. I declined and said to Dad that we would manage. Dad said, "Just call me sometime tonight to let me know that you are safe."

Late that night Keith and I had only made it about one-fifth the way to Montreal. Keith's older brother Angus and a couple of his friends miraculously found Keith and me at a pool hall in Buckingham. Angus had a premonition and just drove there. What were the odds? Buckingham was about 40 kilometres away and we literally could have ended up anywhere. The next day Keith got a haircut.

I left home when I was 19. I would often take some time to visit with Dad, mostly by dropping in on him at the university. Dad confided in me that he had started watching the soap opera "Another World" and admitted to being somewhat addicted to the program. He showed me how he had rigged up a switch to the door of his lab that would automatically turn off the TV set when anyone opened the door. By doing so he was safe to watch that soap opera in secret in his lab during work hours.

When we were children, Dad did not speak much about the war. I do remember things like him looking at a plane with the sun in his eyes. Later on, he would let me know that he was just keeping up his fighter pilot training skills; there is a certain way to look towards the sun and not be blinded by it so that a fighter pilot flying directly into the sun would not experience a disadvantage and a pilot could make out an enemy aircraft even approaching directly from the sun.

As I became older, Dad would open up to me more about the war. I stared calling Dad every November 11, Remembrance Day, to thank him for his service. My siblings and daughters also made this a yearly ritual. Dad was always appreciative of that.

Some of the fondest moments in my life, however, happened during the year that I spent with Dad and Heather at their home in Ottawa as I was interviewing Dad for this book. I am forever grateful that I did that and managed to share all those special moments with him.

Although he suffered through two heart attacks, bypass surgery, and prostate cancer, and even though Dad outlived my kid brother Leo, and my sister Anna-Lee, Heather and Dad enjoyed a fulfilling and rewarding life together. They bought a house in Ottawa's west end and lived there for 10 happy years until Dad felt it was time to move into a retirement residence, Riverpark Place. He lived there with Heather for a few more years until, at age 88, he developed brain cancer. He refused more treatments, and on August 15, 2011, Dad died peacefully in his bed with his beloved Heather by his side.

Heather Pigden Halpern and Joseph Halpern at home in Ottawa

ACKNOWLEDGEMENTS

Thanks Dad, for living such an inspiring life, for all your patient storytelling and for your help with writing Chapter 1.

Thanks to Heather Pigden-Halpern, my stepmother, for her years of devotion to my father, her unmitigated dedication to this book, and her constant support of me. Also, thanks to Heather for her fact-finding and writing the initial version of the chapter "The Kitten of the Volga" and for her work in the "Ambrosia" and "Cigarettes Can Save Your Life" chapters, which include some of her writing.

A special thank you must be given to Rebecca Garber of Wordworks in Nanaimo, British Columbia for her developmental editing, time and research, suggestions, final editing and proof-reading, and help in writing the synopsis. A special acknowledgment goes to Rebecca Garber for creating the title *From School to Sky: Joseph's Tale of War*. Thank you Rebecca for always answering the phone. Without her unrelenting support, inclusion of peers and contacts, this project could not have come to fruition. Rebecca has been utterly amazing!

I must also thank Sylvia McConnell for her editing.

Thanks to spiritual leader Rabbi David Mivasair for his patient and tireless input into the information about Reb Shlomo Halevi Halpern, his work, and his ancestors—and their role in the Judaic history of Warsaw throughout centuries. Rabbi Mivasair also contributed to the chapter "Your Future Country Needs You."

Thank you, Elinor Florence for your support, encouragement and advice.

Thanks to Gloria Luk for her support.

Thank you, Patricia Derouin, who remained my mother's one close friend during all her years of mental health challenges and who became a kind of second mother to us Halpern children.

Thanks also to my brother David and my deceased siblings, Anna-Lee, Leo, and Saul, for their role in Joseph's and my lives.

And especially, I would like to thank my beloved wife Joan for all she did in order for me to complete this project.

A Personal Note

Recent physiological research, pioneered by Rachel Yehuda, has shown that intergenerational trauma can be inherited. Also, a most trusted and compassionate authority on stress, trauma and mental well-being, Gabor Maté, has written a new book *the Myth of Normal*. I had the pleasure of meeting Dr. Maté in February 2023 at the Vancouver Jewish Book Festival where we were both featured authors. I highly recommend this book.

The experiences of trauma endured by my father and mother by living through war, such as explosions and gunfire, may have passed a survivor skill to me and my siblings: our bodies on hyper-alert and reflexes poised to react quickly to loud noises. My entire life, each time such an occurrence like a sudden loud noise, all the people around me would jump or react as if startled. I never did. I would process such occurrences calmly. I just thought that I had fast reflexes.

Unfortunately, for those like me, living in a so called peaceful and safe environment can cause constant hypervigilance which can ultimately create havoc in our bodies. Our ancestors' emotional experiences can become our own, and few of us ever make the link between our individual issues to those of our families in past generations. The recent research has shown that instead, we believe that we are the source of our own problems; that we are somehow broken and because of this belief, we feel that is why we feel the way we do.

Mounting evidence concludes that the offspring of trauma survivors have a greater risk of anxiety, post-traumatic stress disorder, depression, and even premature death. The offspring of trauma survivors may also be more susceptible to drug or alcohol abuse or dependency. That was my case and that of my siblings. Saul, Leo, and Anna-Lee, all died prematurely, directly or indirectly as a result of substance abuse. My older brother David struggled with and managed to overcome addictions to nasal spray, Tylenol, alcohol, and cocaine. I managed to overcome my cocaine addiction and problems associated with alcohol addiction and am continuing therapy.

Printed in the USA
CPSIA information can be obtained
at www.ICGtesting.com
LVHW011642010524
779055LV00036B/577